How To Talk To Women

The Ultimate Guide

(2 Books in 1)

How to Smoothly Start Conversations, Flirt Like a Pro & Become the Man That Women Want

Dave Perrotta

Table Of Contents

The Last Book You'll Ever Need On How To Talk To Women 1

Book 1: How to Flirt With Women 5

Prologue: The Power of Flirting 6

How to Create the "Spark" That Attracts Her 7

The 4 Keys to Flirting Like a Pro 12

- Part 1: Mastering the Flirty Vibe 12
- Part 2: The Flirting Fundamentals 12
- Part 3: How to Flirt in Key Situations 13
- Part 4: How to Be a Natural at Flirting 13
- Remember: Action is King 13

Part 1: Mastering the Flirty Vibe 15

Buyer Bonus 16

How Women Flirt 17

- How She Approaches You (Without Saying a Word) 17
- How Women Flirt in Person 20
- How Women Flirt Over Text 25
- What Women Need to Feel Attraction 27

The 5 Flirty Mindsets That Make You Irresistible 33

- 1. The World Is My Playground 33
- 2. Rejection Is a Win 35
- 3. I Love Women 36

4. I Am in the Moment 37

5. Acceptance 38

Flirt Like James Bond 41

The Smooth Moves of James Bond 41

The Laid-Back Allure of Dex from The Tao Of Steve 45

The Charm of Jacob in Crazy, Stupid, Love 47

Part 2: The Flirting Fundamentals 51

Where To Meet Women 52

During the Day 52

At Night 58

Online 60

What Good Flirting Looks Like 64

It's Subtle Instead of Blunt 64

It's Playful Instead of Overly Serious 65

It's Self-Assured Instead of Insecure 66

It Adds to the Connection 67

It's Risky...But Not Too Risky 68

The Irresistible Flirting Techniques of Top 5% Men 71

Tonality 71

Teasing 75

Passing Her Tests 76

Misinterpretation 78

Push/Pull 79

Future Projecting 83

Flirty Questions 85

Part 3: How to Flirt in Key Situations 90

How to Flirt When You First Meet Her 91

Situational Openers: Your Environment Is Your Wingman 91

Non-Situational Openers: Straight Shooting 93

Nightlife Openers 94

Weaving In Banter Early On 95

Getting Her Contact Info 97

How to Flirt on Dates 104

The Goals of a First Date 104

Cheap & Simple First Date Ideas 106

Flirting on the First Date 107

Flirting With a Group 115

Reframing the Group Approach 115

Understanding Group Dynamics 116

Flirting During Group Interactions 118

Getting Alone Time with Your Girl 121

Flirting Over Text & Dating Apps 125

The 5 Texting Principles 125

Flirting Over Text Before the First Date 127

Flirting Over Text Three or More Dates In 132

How to Flirt in Online Dating 132

Part 4: How to Be a Natural at Flirting 135

The 10 Raw Skills That Make You Better at Flirting 136

1. Wittiness 136

2. Reduced Self-Monitoring 137

3. Sense of Humor 138
4. Storytelling 138
5. Presence 139
6. Empathy 140
7. Self-Amusement 140
8. Self-Acceptance 140
9. Leading 141
10. Spontaneity 142

How to Build the Raw Flirting Skills and Become a Natural with Women 145

Stand-Up Comedy & Improv 145
Freestyle Rapping & Word Association 148
Dance Classes 152
Sitting in Silence 153
Reading Fiction & Non-Fiction 154
Going for the Close 155
Consistent Action 156

Final Thoughts 159

Need Some Extra Help? 162

Book 2: Conversation Casanova 163

(The New & Improved Edition) 163

Prologue: Straight Talk 164

"How Does He Make It Look So Easy?" 165

How to Master Conversation 168

Part 1: The Casanova Mindsets That Drive Her Wild 170

Why Your Mindsets Are Crucial 171

Taking Responsibility for Your Life 173

Overcoming the Need for Validation 177

A Man With Purpose 180

She's Into Me 183

5 More Key Mindsets To Crush It On Your Dating Journey 186

1. There's Always Another One Coming 186

2. Be Careful Who You Listen To 187

3. Try "Cringe-Level" Hard 188

4. Even Keeled: Don't Get Too High Or Too Low 189

5. Fix the Problem By Fixing It! 190

Part 2: Becoming a Top-Tier Man 193

Building a Premium Brand: Your "Girl-Getting Machine" 194

What it Takes to Be a "Catch" in the Modern Dating Market 195

Your "Girl-Getting Machine" 201

What To Do When You're Scared To Talk To Girls 206

Is Approaching Women Even Worth It? 206

How to Overcome The Fear of Approaching 207

Part 3: Initiate The Conversation 214

5 Ways to Start a Conversation With Any Girl 215

1. Going Direct 216

2. Situational 217

3. The "Where is Starbucks?" Approach 218

4. The Simple Introduction 219

5. The Opinion Opener 219

What to Say After You Start the Conversation 222

The Easy Assumption 223

The First Question 223

How to Take Her on an "Instant Date" 227

Part 4: Connect 229

Get Her Talking 230

Get Past the Small Talk and Connect With Her 231

Asking the Right Questions 232

Why Questions Are Important 233

How to Structure Your Questions 234

Listening & Relating 235

Avoiding Common Conversation Mistakes 237

5 Go-To Conversation Topics for Connecting 244

1. Her Experiences 244

2. Her Dreams 245

3. What She Loves to Do 246

4. Her Passions 247

5. Her Motivations 248

Part 5: Captivate 250

Talking About Yourself in an Attractive Way 251

They Focus on Facts & Stats Over Emotions 251

Most Men Are Terrible Storytellers 252

Most Men Don't Convey the Right Qualities About Themselves 252

They Give Away Too Much Too Quickly 252

Step #1: Understand the Purpose of Talking About Yourself 253

Step #2: Highlight Attractive Qualities About Yourself 254

Step #3: Bait Her 260

Step #4: Follow the Proper Etiquette 264

How to Tell a Kick-Ass Story That Hooks Her 269

It Should Help You Connect With Her 274

It Should Showcase Your Attractive Qualities 274

It Should Be About Something She's Interested In 274

It Should End With a Bang 275

Part 6: Relationships, Compatibility & Maintaining A Masculine Frame 279

Casual or Serious: You Still Need a Gameplan 280

Pacing: What Most Guys Get Wrong 283

What Guys Get Wrong About Pacing 283

How to Pace Things Correctly 284

Transitioning to a Relationship 285

How to Know If She's "Girlfriend Material" For You 287

The Chemistry Check 287

The Compatibility Check 288

Paying Attention to Red Flags 289

Maintaining a Masculine Frame & Setting Boundaries 291

The Importance of a Masculine Frame 292

Components of a Strong Masculine Frame 293

Challenges in Maintaining Your Frame 296

Strengthening Your Frame 298

Final Thoughts 300

Epilogue: Your Dream Woman is ____ 302

Counting on You ____ 302

Don't Accept Your Excuses ____ 302

Value Real Connection Over Conquest ____ 303

Constantly Cultivate Your Edge ____ 303

The Journey Is the Reward ____ 304

A Parting Gift ____ 305

About the Author ____ 306

Can You Do Me a Favor? ____ 307

The Last Book You'll Ever Need On How To Talk To Women

The dating game has changed.

The pretty girl at the bar used to be just that—the pretty girl at the bar. Sure, she had some suitors—maybe the guy at work or a few chaps in her social circle.

But now? She might have a *few hundred* guys in her Instagram or dating app inbox pining to wine her and dine her, or even a guy from across the country looking to fly her out. As tech and social media have taken over the world, they've taken over the dating scene, too, and there's much more competition than there used to be.

I don't say all this to scare you or to be "doom and gloom," but instead to show you the potential opportunity that lies ahead.

What this means for you is that there are more guys out there vying for women's attention than ever before. But here's the silver lining: The quality of that competition, at least outside of the top 5% to 10% of guys, is dismally low.

The reason? There's a massive effort gap.

Most guys don't optimize their physical appearance or their online presence, nor do they build high-level social skills or create a life that women would love to be a part of. And it's not that they're not trying hard enough—because to be honest, most guys aren't trying at all.

In fact, many guys have given up on dating altogether—instead, they look out onto the dating landscape and feel like there's no point in even trying.

But it doesn't have to be that way for *you*.

If you're willing to put some effort in, toss your excuses to the side, and be intentional about your dating and social life, you can quickly catapult yourself into that top tier of men that women yearn for.

In fact, the exact strategies I lay out in this book have helped thousands of my coaching clients do just that. They've used these techniques to become the top men in their cities, line up dates with ease, and keep women attracted throughout the dating process. This has allowed them to date from a place of abundance rather than scarcity, accelerating the process of meeting their dream partners.

Most of all, instead of having to "settle," they're able to date women they're truly excited about. And I'm guessing that's why *you're* here, too.

That said, the journey isn't a simple one. You'll need to face rejection, take risks, and challenge your own insecurities. There might also be some tightly held beliefs about women, dating, and even yourself that you need to question.

But if you want to fulfill your potential as a man, there's no other choice. The path must be walked.

I know more than anyone that it's not easy to do alone—and that's exactly why I'm here to guide you along in the process.

Why do I care so much? Because it pains me to see guys not hitting their potential and living lives of frustration. Hell, I used to *be* that guy and it took me a long time to break the cycle. When so many men are "down bad," it hurts society as a whole, weakens relationships, and makes progress harder overall.

This book is my way of doing what's in my power to help—of laying out everything I've learned over my years of coaching thousands of guys, dating amazing women, and making countless mistakes.

I'm just a guy that tried "cringe-level" hard at dating for over a decade who's looking to make it a lot easier for the guys that come after me.

If you're onboard with that and enjoy a no-nonsense, no-BS approach to things, then this is the book for you. Let's get ready to roll.

We'll start with Book 1 – *How to Flirt With Women.*

It'll show you everything you need to know to attract and flirt with the ladies you're excited about. From starting flirty conversations and keeping them going to handling yourself on dates and more, this book will cover the gamut.

It'll teach you how to have flirty, fun, and engaging conversations with women rather than the boring and platonic interactions that plague most guys' efforts.

Next, we'll transition to Book 2 – *Conversation Casanova (The New & Improved Edition).*

This book will help you master your conversation skills in a broader sense, make deeper connections, and become the type of man that women go crazy for.

It'll also show you how to navigate the dating process, from the initial meetup to the first few dates and right up until you're in a healthy, long-term relationship.

The original *Conversation Casanova*, which I published back in 2016, has sold over 80,000 copies. This is the newly updated edition—I've removed the fluff and added over 10,000 words of new content, examples, and strategies to help you master dating in the modern era. So even if you've read the book before, you'll get a ton of value out of this new edition.

And even if you're brand new to my content, we're going to have some fun. If you've followed me for a while on Instagram or my YouTube channel, think of this as my magnum opus of dating. While that might seem a little smug, as I'll teach you in both of these books, confidence is everything.

Without further ado, let's get started with Book 1.

Book 1

How to Flirt With Women

Discover How to Talk to Women, Never Run Out of Things to Say & Master the Art of Seduction

Prologue: The Power of Flirting

How to Create the "Spark" That Attracts Her

You just got home from an amazing first date. Everything went right. She was beautiful. She laughed at your jokes. The two of you connected. And the entire time, you were thinking, "I could really see myself with this girl!"

You walk back home feeling a sense of giddy, excited energy and can't help but think of the future. Date two, three, and beyond. Settling in at home, you send her a text: "Hey, Emily. I hope you got home safe! Tonight was a lot of fun."

And then?

Crickets.

You don't hear back from Emily until later the next day. But when you read her text, your stomach drops. "Hey, I had fun too! I don't want to waste your time though. I didn't feel a spark, and I don't see this going anywhere. Good luck with everything!"

You put your phone down and let out a sigh. "This is the fourth time something like this has happened in the last couple of months," you explain to your friend. "I'm tired of it, and I don't know what's going wrong!"

Sound familiar?

Maybe you've also had dates where she "didn't feel a spark," or interactions where you thought that all went well but then she ghosted you when you asked to hang out.

Or maybe you've put dating off for a long time and haven't had many opportunities to get out there and meet women who you're excited about.

Whatever the case, there's one missing piece that you need in order to get past these obstacles and attract your ideal kind of woman: the ability to flirt!

So, what exactly *is* flirting?

In short, it's the unspoken language of attraction.

It's the sly, back-and-forth subtleties where you don't necessarily come right out and say, "Hey, I'm into you!" Instead, think of it as kind of a secret conversation that goes on below the surface of what's being said.

It's a mix of playful banter, innuendos, teasing looks, and a magnetic vibe that excites both you and the beautiful woman on the other side of the table. It's a fun way of showing interest and expressing romantic intent.

The men who can master this secret language of flirting move through their dating lives with ease. Their conversations flow effortlessly, women chase them, and they hardly ever get that dreaded "I didn't feel a spark" text. In fact, usually they're the ones who have to send that text to the women, as their many dating options have allowed them to have higher standards.

Why do you need to master it?

Every truly top-tier man speaks the language of flirting fluently, as do most women.

When you have the ability to flirt, you can connect with ease, make great first impressions, create a "spark" with a woman, and make any interaction or date more fun and memorable.

It's truly an art that grants you admission to the world of women. It allows you to be "the guy" who she giggles over and gets excited about with her friends.

And it gives you the ability to strut into any room with confidence, knowing that even the most beautiful woman in the room could be just one conversation or even one look away from giving you her number and setting up a date.

You become a man with confidence, options, and abundance—something most men will never truly experience. These options also allow you to date different women, understand what you like and don't like, and choose a high-quality partner without having to settle.

It also makes for some pretty awesome first dates!

But in contrast, if you never truly master flirting, you'll feel like you're navigating a perpetual solo dance floor, where the music plays but you're standing on the sidelines, unsure of how to join in.

You'll see other guys having success and dating the women they want, and you'll feel left out or like you're "falling behind." You'll miss connections and opportunities with the women you were most excited about and wonder "What could've been."

Overall, you won't be able to fully express yourself to potential mates and life will be less fun.

I know this fate all too well—I've worked with many guys who come from this world where flirting is a foreign language, and I also dealt with it myself for many years before I finally figured things out. But now I can see just how much things can transform once you become fluent.

Now here's the good news:

Any man can master the art of how to flirt with women.

Whether you're wealthy or struggling financially, naturally charismatic or shy, conventionally attractive or "not naturally good looking," you can absolutely learn this essential skill and apply it in your life.

And in this book, you'll discover exactly how to do just that. You'll no longer have to be on the outside looking in.

It's time to join the party and embrace the adventure that awaits you once you tap into your potential and unleash your true flirting abilities.

But before we dive in, you're likely wondering, "Who is this guy and what does he know about flirting and seduction?" Fair question. I get it. After all, there's a ton of shady characters out there on social media these days preaching questionable advice.

My name is Dave Perrotta, and I've dedicated the last thirteen years of my life to mastering the dating skillset. First (and obviously) for my own sake, and then through coaching thousands of men to do the same.

I started as an insecure guy in my early twenties with no idea how to talk to women or speak the language of flirting. This lack of dating success frustrated me so much that it embedded a deep desire within me to get this part of my life fully handled. And that's exactly what I did, although it took me several years and several thousands of approaches and dates.

But as I transformed my dating life, I saw the rest of my life change, too. Once I could conquer my fear of talking to that cute girl, no fear in my life was off limits. This led me on an epic adventure—I went on to quit my desk job, live in over 20 countries, and start multiple online businesses. And it also inspired me to give back and help other men make the same transformation in *their* dating lives.

You may have seen me on Instagram, TikTok, or YouTube—where I have over 400,000 combined followers—or heard about one of my bestselling books like *Conversation Casanova*.

Over the years, I've worked with men from all walks of life. From 19-year-old guys who've barely ever talked to a girl, 30-somethings who are trying to balance their dating and professional life, and even 60-somethings coming out of decades-long marriages, as well as everyone in between.

I've seen it all. I've come face to face with the mindsets and conversation struggles that hold men back, and I have a deep understanding of how to get you past them. That's what this book is all about. Once you master the art of flirting by following the essential tips and techniques within these pages, your dating life won't be filled with frustration but instead with abundance and fulfillment. You'll have a clear path and plan to attract your ideal partner.

The 4 Keys to Flirting Like a Pro

This book is divided into four key parts that'll help you master the art of flirting. I suggest reading the chapters in order, as each part will help you understand the next. Then, once you've read the entire book, you can go back and review the material that centers around your biggest sticking points.

Part 1: Mastering the Flirty Vibe

This section gives you a deeper understanding of flirting. You'll discover flirting from the woman's perspective so that you'll know what she's attracted to and what signs she'll give off when she likes you. You'll also internalize the key flirting mindsets—without these, every flirting technique will be just a facade. But once you internalize these mindsets, flirting will be a natural part of the way you operate as a man. Then we'll look at some movie examples and breakdowns to help you understand and witness effective flirting in action, along with how to replicate it yourself.

Part 2: The Flirting Fundamentals

In this section, you'll discover the building blocks of flirting with and meeting attractive women.

We'll cover where to meet them in your everyday life and online, how to get the conversation started, and the actual techniques to flirt with and attract women.

Afterwards, you'll have a toolbox full of great flirting techniques to help you master the art of seduction and never run out of things to say.

Part 3: How to Flirt in Key Situations

You'll discover exactly how to flirt with women—when you first meet her, when you're on a date or in a group, and when you're texting or messaging on dating apps.

Whatever situation you might come across, you'll know exactly how to break out the flirting techniques, lead things forward, and get her interested.

Part 4: How to Be a Natural at Flirting

You don't want to have to keep referring back to a book every time you want to flirt with a girl, right? You want flirting to feel natural—to the point where it feels effortless to charm the ladies like a pro.

That's the point of this section, in which I'll uncover the ten raw skills that'll make you a natural at flirting. These are the exact skills I teach my dating coaching clients—the same skills I used to use myself to effortlessly flirt on the way to meeting my amazing girlfriend. Finally, you'll discover how to easily build these raw flirting skills with a set of small daily habits that'll only take you a few months to master. Once you get these down, your flirting will flow smoothly and effortlessly.

Remember: Action is King

If you truly want to succeed with flirting and attract the women of your dreams, you've got to take consistent action.

Simply reading books, watching YouTube videos, and listening to podcasts isn't going to cut it. There are no "magic" solutions out there—and this book isn't one either. But if you're ready to take your dating life and flirting abilities seriously, it *will* give you all the tools to succeed. So absorb these words, apply what you learn, and then get ready to embark on an awesome new journey where (unlike so many other guys out there) you'll actually have control over your dating life.

Part 1: Mastering the Flirty Vibe

Buyer Bonus

As my way of saying thank you, I'm offering my **Dating Mastery Bundle** that includes five FREE downloads exclusive to my book readers.

Here's what you'll get:

1. **The First Date Playbook:** A cheat sheet for first date success with conversation starters, key questions to ask, and tips on creating a memorable experience.
2. **Get a Girlfriend in 30 Days - Audio Guide:** The extensive step-by-step audio guide to meeting, attracting, and dating your dream girl in 30 days or less.
3. **5 Texting Mistakes that Destroy Attraction - Audio Guide:** Discover the texting mistakes that turn her off, derail her attraction, and make you look needy.
4. **The Approach Anxiety Buster PDF:** This guide shows you exactly how to work through your anxiety and confidently start conversations with beautiful women.
5. **The Top-Tier Dating Profile Kickstart:** This resource shows you how to get attractive photos and increase your matches by five to ten times on dating apps—and attract women on Instagram, too.

Download your bonuses here:

Go to **daveperrotta.com/mastery** or scan the QR code below.

How Women Flirt

To become great at flirting yourself, you first must understand how *women* flirt. And we've all been there. You're talking to a girl or she catches your eye from across the room, or maybe she just sends you an interesting text, and you think, "Is she flirting with me? Was that laugh platonic...or something more?

When you understand how women flirt, you'll quickly pick up on their cues and be able to tell what's working—as well as what's *not* working.

The nuances of her body language, the tone of her voice, the subtleties of her expressions, and the words she says (and texts) can all let you know exactly where you stand in the interaction. When you're able to read these signals correctly, you'll have effortless conversations without any overthinking and calibrate your advances more smoothly.

Compare this to the average guy, who might as well be a deer in the headlights when attempting to flirt with a woman. He may pick up on her signs some of the time, but that's more luck than skill—and luck isn't repeatable so it won't help you much in the long run. Let's first examine how women flirt in person, and then we'll cover the nuances of how they flirt over text.

How She Approaches You (Without Saying a Word)

First, you need to understand that women live in a slightly different world than us guys. We can go up and talk to a girl and get rejected, and it's not a big deal.

We may *think* that it's a big deal, but no one really bats an eye in the grand scheme of things. We don't actually risk that much, because it's socially acceptable—and even expected—for the man to initiate things.

However, from a woman's point of view, approaching a man generally *is* a big deal. If she goes up and gets rejected in front of everyone, it'll feel much harder to live down for her than it is for us. It's not as socially acceptable and so it's more of a social risk. That's why women won't often approach you first—even if you're dressed to the nines with all the "game" in the world and all your fundamentals on point. But women, as crafty as they are, have outsmarted us men.

They've figured out a way to approach us without any of the social risk that comes along with getting rejected. They don't need to say a single word, and the men who are "tuned in" know exactly what's going on.

How do they do this? Through something called an "approach invitation." This is where she subtly lets you know that she's interested and gives you an opportunity to come up and talk to her—and then it's on *you* to make your move. And you'd better act fast because if the window closes, you'll likely lose your chance (or another guy may catch on and swoop in). **Below are some of the most common approach invitations women will give you:**

- She'll look at you and smile (even from across the room)
- She'll look in your general direction multiple times for no apparent reason
- She'll position herself nearby you, also for no apparent reason
- She'll pass close by and maybe even brush against you

- She'll ask you an innocent question (if you have any drink recommendations or even for directions)

If she gives you these signs and you like what you see, don't be afraid to move in and go talk to her! But all too often, guys overlook even the most obvious approach invitations. They'll think, "She's probably not looking at me" or "I'm not sure what to say to her anyway," and do nothing. Don't be one of these guys. Instead, just assume that she's attracted to you and then go find out for yourself. I remember one time in Budapest when I was walking through a street of crowded restaurant patios. A beautiful girl caught my eye from about 15 feet away, and I saw her smile. I walked through the restaurant, approached her table, and started a quick conversation. I invited her and her friends to come out with us later that night—they agreed, met us a few hours later, and we had a great time. All from one initial glance from a distance!

These approach invitations are powerful because they allow you to make a "warm approach" (like you already have some familiarity) rather than a "cold approach" (in which the two of you haven't acknowledged each other yet). There's already an expected and assumed level of attraction, especially if you've both made eye contact and smiled. This makes things easier for you.

Now, you won't *always* get these invitations from girls you want to talk to. Often, and especially as you get started on improving, you won't, and so you've got to be prepared to start conversations from scratch. And that's just fine—some of your best conversations will happen this way. I've dated many girls who never gave me an approach invitation at the start.

But just because she hasn't given you an approach invitation doesn't mean she hasn't noticed you—some women just shy away from giving these invitations.

Now you might be wondering, "How do I get more of these approach invitations?"

In short, the better you look and the better you're positioned, the more it will happen. **Here's what you can do to get more women looking your way:**

- Looksmaxx. In other words, optimize your "good looking" potential by improving your style, getting a good haircut, fixing your teeth, building muscle, and having clear skin. When you look good, women will notice.

- Have solid, open posture and a relaxed facial expression. The more laid back and receptive you look, the more inviting you'll appear to women who'd like to meet you.

- Master your positioning. If you see a cute girl in a cafe, sit near her. If you're going for a walk, do so in higher traffic areas where more women can pass by. And if you're out at night, stand in a place where the most women can see you.

How Women Flirt in Person

Now let's shift to what happens when you're actually talking to a woman. Understanding how she flirts will help you to read women better—as well as become better at flirting yourself.

Eye Contact

Women can basically speak an entire language with their eyes.

They won't just use their eyes to draw you in and get you to approach them but *also* while they're in a conversation with you.

First, you've got the "doggy dinner bowl" eyes. She'll give you this look when she's super into you and eating up everything you say. Her pupils dilate, her eyebrows raise, and her eyes become wide. She wants more and it's very obvious that she's into you. When you get this, it's time to kiss her or take whatever the next step is, like going to a more private location where intimacy might be possible.

Another thing to watch for is prolonged eye contact. When girls aren't interested, they tend to glance away often and avoid giving you their full attention. But when she's fully locked in and staring right into your eyes for most of the conversation, odds are that she's highly interested.

Then you've got the "eye contact, smile, and look down" combo. This can happen when she notices you from across the room, or even in a conversation with you. It often indicates that she's being flirty but also a little shy and bashful.

What She Says

Women's flirting certainly isn't all non-verbal–they flirt with their words too. It's a good sign if she's doing any of the following:

Playful Teasing

Maybe she pokes fun at your favorite music or TV show, or even teases you about a story that you shared. Or, while she does this, maybe she gives you a little playful nudge on the arm.

She might even bring up an inside joke about something that came up earlier in the conversation.

This is her way of showing you that she's comfortable enough around you to make jokes and invite you into her world a little bit. Be aware of this and you won't be an "outsider" like the majority of men who "don't get it" when it comes to women.

Compliments

If she's flirting, she might not be able to resist throwing a compliment or two at you. Maybe she mentions how she loves your smile, the color of your eyes, or even just the fact that you can make her laugh.

All of these are good signs. She's unlikely to compliment guys she's not into, right?

Innuendos

She might make up her own innuendos or just respond very positively when you weave one into the conversation. Again, this is her way of bringing you "in on the joke" and seeing if you can play ball with some fun banter of your own.

Testing You

Women's tests are another form of flirting. She might say things like, "Do you say this to every girl?", "You know we're not sleeping together, right?", "Do you really like that kind of music?", and so on.

She's testing to see how you respond and if you're really the guy you make yourself out to be. A lot of guys put on facades, and she wants to make sure that you're not one of them. That's why it's actually a good thing if she tests you—it shows that she wants you to be "that" guy. And if you pass, you're in.

Future Plans

As she becomes more enamored with you, she might start future-projecting things that the two of you could do together: "I've been wanting to see that show for so long. We should go together!" "So, you like to cook pizza? I'll have to see that for myself!"

She's finding ways to envision spending more time with you.

Lots of Questions

When she's interested, she'll want to know a lot about you. She might pelt you with questions about your life, interests, and dreams.

She's not just making small talk—she's aiming to get to know the real you.

Physical Flirting

Women flirt physically, too, through touch and other ways.

She might initiate some of those playful touches mentioned previously after making a joke or teasing you—maybe even a brief hand on the chest while laughing. She's looking to establish a connection and gauge your reaction.

You can initiate this first, too, and see how she reacts. One of my favorite moves on a first date is after leaving the venue and I put my arm around her. If she's warm and leans right into me, I know there's very high interest, and I can give her a quick kiss right then and there as I lead things to the next location.

Then there's physical mirroring, which is a subconscious behavior that indicates rapport and attraction. If she's mimicking your gestures, posture, and movements, she might just be into you.

And perhaps the easiest one to be aware of is proximity. The more she leans into you, the closer she stands, and the more she gets into your "bubble" and allows you into hers, the more she's likely interested. Be aware of her subtle body language cues as well. Is she leaning toward you? Are her feet squarely pointed in your direction while she maintains open posture? These are all great signs.

And one of my favorites to test all this out? Give her a high five during a high point in the conversation. If she clasps your hand with her fingers, there's definite high interest there.

Following Your Lead

In general, if a woman follows your lead, it means that she likes where things are going.

The two examples above—the high five with the hand clasp and the arm around her with the lean in—exhibit this.

You should always be looking to move things forward as early as you can in the interaction to test her interest level.

For example, if you meet her at the bar, you can move her a few feet over to get out of the way of foot traffic. If you meet her during the day, you can give her a handshake and hold it for a few seconds longer than normal and see if she follows along.

Then, as you get more buy-in and investment from her, you can go for bigger and bigger asks, from a kiss to eventually going back to somewhere more intimate.

Dressing To Impress

How does she show up to meet you? This is always a tell-tale sign when it comes to first dates.

If she shows up in sweats with a disheveled appearance, she definitely doesn't have much of a stake in the date. But if she comes dressed to impress with heels, a nice dress, her hair done, and flawless makeup, there's zero doubt that she's interested and sees this as a date.

How Women Flirt Over Text

Now you've got a great understanding of how women flirt in person. But over text? That's a different story, and it's where many guys get confused (and eventually ghosted). They don't know how to pick up on her flirting. Let's solve this below.

The Extended Word

This has been women's go-to flirting method since texting was invented. A prime example? "Heyyyy"—the more "y"s at the end, the higher her interest level. She also might throw in a "Lmaoooo" or a "Hahahaha," which are other frequent forms of extended phrases.

Lots of Emojis

As a man, you don't want to overuse emojis—and you *definitely* don't want to use them more than she does. Why? Because it can make you come across a little too eager, needy, or even feminine. But emojis are a woman's bread and butter when it comes to flirting over text, and the more of these she uses, the more it signals that she's into you.

Voice Messages

I've noticed that this is more of a thing with Latina and Spanish women. They love to send long voice notes in Spanish with a ton of slang (and I have to listen to them ten times so I'm sure of the meaning). Voice notes are becoming a little more common in America too, though. And as you'll learn later in the book, you can use them to your advantage. Generally, though, she won't take the time to make a voice message unless she's at least somewhat into you, so just the fact that she's sending you one is a good sign.

Exclamation Points

Women love to spice things up with some extra exclamation points when they're trying to flirt. Just like with the extended word, the more of these she throws in, the more excited she is about talking to you.

Response Time

A lot of guys get wrapped up in judging a woman's response time in their text conversations. And that's fair enough, because it does matter. If she takes hours (or days) to respond, it means that she's probably got something else tying up her attention—perhaps even another guy. This isn't always the case, and if she's usually down to hang out, you don't need to read too much into it—especially early on.

But if you're several dates in, you've gotten intimate already, and she's *still* taking a long time to respond? There's a good chance that she might not see you as more than a hookup buddy.

Because when she's highly invested and interested in you, her response times should generally either mirror yours or be even quicker.

What Women Need to Feel Attraction

Simply put, if you don't know what generates attraction in women, they won't try to flirt with you. So let's take a look at a few key factors that generate this attractiveness and make her go wild for you.

Strong Communication & Flirting Skills

Being able to talk and flirt confidently is a must in the dating world. You can max out your potential in every other area and make yourself into a "great package," but if you can't communicate and flirt, it won't matter. You won't be able to market yourself or make her feel positive emotions.

This is why there are so many men who are successful with their careers and finances but can't attract or hold down a quality woman.

This is also why a guy like me, when I was in my early twenties and completely broke, had much more dating success than the doctors, lawyers, and other wealthier guys I hung out with.

Once you've mastered flirting, everything else becomes much easier.

Capability & Competence

Women love a man who's capable, competent, and can handle anything that's thrown his way.

They toss a verbal jab or a test at him? He can pass it no problem.

An issue comes up in his business? He can figure it out.

Whether it's excelling in your career or mastering a hobby, showing competence signals to a woman that you're dependable and can provide stability in a relationship. It's also just plain sexy for her to see you do something really well, like mastering the intricacies of a fun and flirty conversation.

Confidence

Hey, I know that you don't need to read a book on flirting to understand that women love confidence, but it's still important to point out!

Confidence is like a magnet that draws women in. It's about knowing who you are and what you bring to the table without coming across as arrogant. When you have confidence, it shows that you're comfortable in your own skin and not afraid to go after what you want. It's that inner strength and self-assurance that make a man irresistible to women.

What's interesting is that the more capable and competent you become, the more confident you become as well. It comes with repetition, so get those reps in!

Warmth

You want there to be an element of warmth to your personality and flirting. Women *love* this. It makes them feel that you're "in this together" and that you're different from other guys. It makes them feel like the two of you are on the same team.

To give off a sense of warmth, you need a mix of the following:

- **Authenticity:** This comes down to being self-amused and approaching interactions with genuine interest, sincerity, and openness.

- **Empathy:** This is the ability to understand and share her feelings. It shows you're attuned to her emotions and fosters a sense of connection.
- **Kindness:** This could be a simple gesture like opening the car door for her, handling the bill on a date, or walking her home.
- **Approachability:** It's all about having an open and friendly demeanor that makes others feel comfortable in your presence.
- **Positive Energy:** This is a mix of having a sense of hopefulness in the future and intentionally putting yourself in a positive mental state.
- **Good Intentions:** You need to have genuinely good intentions for every woman you meet. No bitterness—just the willingness to have a good experience and add some sort of value rather than extract it.

Essentially, when you have warmth, she can feel that you genuinely want the best for her. She knows that you're not going to do anything creepy or weird and that she can have a good level of trust in you.

The more of this she feels, the more she'll open up and want to go on adventures with you. It also gives her the freedom to show you her "secret side"—the side of her that nobody else really ever gets to see. This is when her walls completely go down, and it's a beautiful thing. You get the privilege of experiencing her in her genuine, most authentic form, which lays the groundwork for an incredibly deep connection.

When you really have this dialed in, women can show you more in a single interaction than they've shown to serious boyfriends they've had in the past. You'll hear a lot of, "I've never said this to anyone before" and "I feel like I can be myself around you." And she won't be saying these things in a platonic way, either.

Self-Awareness

There are a lot of people out there who basically go through their entire lives as drones. They live an unexamined existence and never really know themselves. Remember that your level of self-awareness becomes apparent very quickly in your interactions with women.

Women are attracted to men who know themselves well—men who reflect on their actions but also their inner thoughts, feelings, and motivations.

Here's how to be more self-aware:

- **Practice Mindfulness:** Try things like meditation, deep breathing exercises, or simply taking a few moments each day to pause and check in with yourself.
- **Reflect on Your Values and Beliefs:** What matters most to you and why? Aligning your actions with your values can help you live a more authentic life.
- **Seek Feedback:** Ask trusted friends, family members, or mentors for honest feedback about your strengths and areas for improvement. Be open to that feedback (even if it ruffles your feathers a bit) and use it as an opportunity for growth.
- **Journaling:** Keep a journal to document your thoughts, emotions, and experiences. Writing can be a powerful tool for self-reflection and self-

discovery, even if you just jot out some thoughts for five to ten minutes at the beginning or end of your day.

Above all, you need to realize that nobody has it all figured out—and that you're no exception to the rule. Always be open to learning, getting better, and taking in feedback.

Now, if we step back and look at each of these five traits we've just examined, we can see that they'll help you show women a good time in the moment but also give them confidence in your long-term potential. Developing these qualities gives you a big edge over other guys in the dating marketplace, and it allows you to have much more control over your dating life.

Key Takeaways

- **Awareness:** You now understand the woman's perspective on things, as well as how she actively and subconsciously flirts with you. This will make it obvious if your flirting attempts are working (or falling flat).

- **Approach Invitations:** Be aware of these, as they're her way of approaching you without actually doing so. When you get an invitation, move in fast before the window closes.

- **Body Language and Verbal Cues:** Pay attention to the signals she's giving—this will give you a good read on where the interaction is currently at and how quickly you may be able to move things to the next step.

- **Be Aware of Her Texting:** Extended words, lots of emojis and exclamation points, and fast response times convey interest and excitement.

- **Up Your Game:** Build out the traits and qualities that attract women—strong communication and flirting skills, competence and capability, confidence, warmth, and self-awareness.

The 5 Flirty Mindsets That Make You Irresistible

Good flirting starts in the mind. Flirty, attractive men think differently than the average guy. You might even say that they have a unique approach to life and a fresh perspective on dating and women.

Plus, the right mindset can transform flirting from a nerve-wracking experience into a confident and enjoyable interaction.

Let's examine the five most important flirting mindsets that'll make you stand out among all the other guys and become irresistible to women.

1. The World Is My Playground

Picture a guy who approaches dating with a rigid and serious mindset. He sees every interaction with a woman as a test of his worthiness and whether or not he's truly "good enough." He constantly worries about screwing up and feels like he needs to perform at the top of his game at all times. In short, rejection terrifies him.

He doesn't see the world as a playground—he sees it as a battlefield. He's so hyperfocused on his own insecurities and shortcomings that he can't just let go and have fun. And he wouldn't *dream* of showing vulnerability or taking unnecessary social risks, as this might make him seem weak and inadequate.

Do you see the problem here? He's so concerned about how he looks and whether he's good enough that he comes across as stiff and insecure around women. And this is a *major* turnoff. As a result, his attempts at flirting feel contrived and fall flat.

This is how many men approach flirting, as well as life in general. And it's no surprise—they spend most of their days with this mindset, approaching their career or job like a battlefield. It's hard to adjust when it comes to interacting with women.

But let me offer a contrast to this.

Imagine yourself as a kid again, stepping foot onto the playground. You look around and see the other kids playing, the jungle gym waiting to be explored, and the sand begging for you to dash around and play tag in it. You've got a sense of wonder and excitement, and the possibilities feel endless.

Now, translate that same mindset into your interactions with women.

Instead of taking yourself so seriously and viewing dating as a high-stakes game in which every move is scrutinized and judged, see it as an opportunity for fun and enjoyment.

You can approach that girl, say that innuendo, and make that joke—you might not know what'll happen but at least it'll be interesting.

Embrace the spontaneity and unpredictability of human connection, just like you'd embrace the twists and turns of a jungle gym or a fun game of tag with your childhood friends.

When you see the world as your playground, flirting becomes effortless and natural. You're not afraid to take risks or make mistakes because, hey—it's all part of the game. You can tease and banter with ease, knowing that it's all in good fun. And if things *don't* go as planned, you simply brush it off and move on to the next adventure.

With this mindset, you can also approach women with genuine curiosity and interest. You no longer view them as potential conquests or obstacles to overcome—instead, you view them as fellow players in the game of life. You're genuinely interested in getting to know them, not just as potential romantic partners but as people with their own fun and unique experiences and stories.

We can take this one step further by looking at it this way: Every time you leave your front door, there's an adventure to be had.

That woman walking by on the sidewalk, the cute cashier at the grocery store, the pretty girl who glances over to you at the gym—any one of them could be your next fun conversation or, who knows, maybe even your next girlfriend. When you have an openness to life rather than that rigid "I'm going about my day and I don't have time to notice or talk to women" mentality, the possibilities become endless.

So be the guy on the playground and embrace your inner childlike wonder. It's all a game anyway, so you might as well get in there and play it and have a little fun!

2. Rejection Is a Win

The men who are best at flirting are able to separate rejection from their own personal self-worth. They understand that not every interaction or date will lead to a positive outcome, and they're okay with that. Instead, they see rejection as an opportunity for growth and self-improvement.

Maybe they talk to a girl, make a joke that falls flat, and realize that they need to be a little more socially calibrated and attentive to social cues. Perhaps they discover that they're not as compatible with certain types of women as they initially thought. This allows them to more quickly filter for women who might actually be a good fit.

After coaching thousands of guys, I can confidently say that the men with this mindset improve astronomically faster than those who get bent out of shape and dwell on every single rejection. Instead of needing to jump a giant mental hurdle of angst and frustration every time a woman ghosts them or brushes off their attempt at a second date, they let it roll right off their shoulders and keep moving along.

This courage in the face of rejection also makes their flirting more smooth. Again, they don't fear risk taking, and so they come off as more fun and with more of an edge than most other guys, which ultimately makes them stand out.

And if you think about it, rejection is actually a *win*. The woman who turned you down saved you time. Instead of having to pine over someone who's uninterested, you have the freedom to move on and meet women who *are* interested, and that's the whole point.

3. I Love Women

A man who's good at flirting must genuinely love women—the two go hand-in-hand. And quite honestly, that's what a lot of these red pill guys don't seem to understand.

A man who genuinely loves women sees them as complex and fascinating instead of prizes to be won. There's a genuine kindness behind everything he does and says, without any kind of ulterior motive or agenda. For him, flirting isn't about manipulating women. It's about being in the moment, enjoying one another's presence, being self-amused, and engaging in the subtle dance of attraction that comes with flirting. He wants to get to know her on a deeper level, have some fun banter, and share unique moments together.

That split second in time when you're locked in with a beautiful woman, totally on the same wavelength, and knowing that you just "get each other"—it's one of the most magical moments this life has to offer.

With these kinds of interactions, there's a big difference between the warm sincerity that comes from a man who loves women compared to the insincere crassness from a man who's bitter about them.

4. I Am in the Moment

Imagine a man who approaches interactions with women with a laser focus on the present. He's fully engaged, attentive, and invested in the conversation, making the woman feel like she's the only thing that matters at that point in time.

He puts aside any distractions and worries, as well as his thoughts about the future or the past. He's even able to put aside what this girl might be thinking of him. His entire focus is on her words, expressions, and body language—everything that encompasses the present interaction.

He doesn't simply wait until it's his turn to speak; he listens intently, asks genuine questions, makes playful teases, and shows authentic curiosity. This allows him to pick up on the subtle nuances in her moods, emotions, and reactions in real-time. This full presence helps him create a sense of intimacy that goes beyond the surface-level small talk she has with every other guy.

She feels like she's experiencing something special and unique with him. It's a memorable encounter, and she wants more.

If you're looking for some sort of a "secret sauce" to flirting, this is it. Every guy who's a natural with women has this down pat. Things are able to flow smoothly and he's fully engaged. Remember—this is a stark contrast for women, who are used to dealing with neurotic, overly analytical men.

We'll examine more about how to be present later in this book. But here's an easy tip: When you talk to a beautiful woman, enjoy it! It's supposed to be fun, not some complicated jigsaw puzzle you struggle to figure out. The relaxed and laid-back presence you embody will easily make you stand out.

5. Acceptance

You've got to be okay with that fact that not every interaction will spark fireworks.

There'll be women with whom you have amazing chemistry with, and over the span of a quick conversation, you'll feel like you've known her for years and you completely click. It's beautiful when this happens but, sadly, it just isn't the case each and every time.

That's because there are levels to chemistry and connection. Some girls you'll click with on an okay level, and this can be sufficient for a casual hookup sort of situation. Then there'll be others where it feels like the connection is a 10/10, and these are your serious relationship potential girls. You still need to test if there's compatibility, but compatibility doesn't matter if there's no chemistry.

But there'll also be times when you do everything right, and for whatever reason, there's just no chemistry there. The conversation feels forced. Maybe she's having a bad day, or maybe your personalities are just completely incompatible.

Think of it this way: Not every person you meet is going to be your new best friend, right? The same goes for romantic connections. You won't click with every girl you flirt with, and that's totally fine.

When you accept this reality, it takes the pressure off. You can relax and enjoy the process without worrying about every interaction needing to lead somewhere. And you know what? It's actually liberating.

Because when you're not desperately trying to force a connection, you come across as more genuine and confident. And that's attractive in itself.

So the next time you're flirting with a girl and things don't quite click, just shrug it off. It's no big deal—there are plenty of more opportunities out there. Just keep improving your flirting fundamentals and confidence, put yourself out there, and you'll meet girls you *do* click with. That's the goal after all, right?

Key Takeaways

- **Embrace Playfulness:** Approach interactions with women with the mindset that the world is your playground. Let go of rigid expectations and see each conversation as an opportunity for fun, enjoyment, and adventure.

- **See Rejection as a Win:** Instead of fearing rejection, regard it as a chance to learn something new, as well as to grow and improve. Rejection allows you to refine your flirting skills and filter for women who are genuinely interested.

- **Cultivate a Genuine Love for Women:** Cut out all the red pill mindsets and develop a sincere love and respect for women. This will help you flirt from a place of warmth, kindness, and good intentions.

- **Be Present:** Be fully there when you interact with women. Listen attentively, ask genuine questions, and show interest in what they're saying.

- **Embrace Acceptance:** You won't click with every girl you meet, and that's totally fine. At the same time, there'll be levels to the chemistry and connection with girls that you do click with.

Flirt Like James Bond: Movie Character Examples to Build Your Flirting Style

If you've never been great at flirting, nor have had any friends who've really mastered it, it can be a challenge to understand what good flirting actually looks like.

But thanks to Hollywood, you don't have to imagine it all on your own. There are a few movie characters who are flirting masters, and there are hard-hitting lessons you can learn from each one and apply to your own flirting methods.

If you haven't seen these movies, it'd be a good idea to check them out—or at least watch a few clips of them on YouTube. **We'll examine three specific characters:**

- James Bond from the classic spy movies
- Dex from The Tao of Steve
- Jacob Palmer from Crazy, Stupid, Love

The Smooth Moves of James Bond

Whenever a coaching client of mine is having a freak out or going into full panic mode about women, I like to reference James Bond.

Bond's got confidence in spades, and he's unfazed even by the most intense of situations. Whether he's facing down a villain or wooing a femme fatale, he never breaks a sweat.

He's also got a knack for witty banter. As is clear in every interaction, he's got a comeback for everything and he can pass any test that women throw his way. Now, bear in mind that you don't need to be a crime-fighting, world-renowned, undercover spy to exhibit these abilities yourself, as we'll see below.

Let's look at a few techniques you can use in your flirting, perfectly demonstrated by Bond.

1. Observation & Adaptability

Remember when we examined how presence is key in your interactions? Bond has this down pat.

He's always attuned to social cues and signals given off by those around him. This allows him to adapt his flirting style to suit the preferences and personality of the woman he's interacting with.

Let's take his encounter with Sévérine in Skyfall as an example (you can check out the clip here: https://bit.ly/skyfall-flirting).

Bond saunters into the casino and locks eyes with her, and she meets his gaze with a mix of apprehension and curiosity. "Now you can afford to buy me a drink," she starts, noticing his winnings.

Bond pauses, looks into her eyes, and says, "Maybe I'll even stretch to two."

Right from the start, their conversation is laced with innuendo and subtle hints of danger. Sévérine, initially guarded, finds herself drawn to Bond's magnetic charisma.

At one point, she's about to leave but Bond gently grabs her forearm and makes an observation. He mentions her tattoo and then calls out her feeling of vulnerability. By doing so, he creates a sense of intimacy between them and lays the groundwork for a stronger connection—as well as more banter and flirting.

This interaction gives a perfect example of passing a woman's test. Instead of getting flustered when she says, "Now you can afford to buy me a drink," Bond stays cool, calm, and collected. He simply agrees and exaggerates a little bit, saying that maybe he can buy her two, and then keeps going unfazed. You can use this in your own interactions.

For example, if a woman says, "You know we're not sleeping together, right?", you could agree and exaggerate with a sly smile before saying, "Of course not. You've got to wine and dine me first!"

2. Leading & Seizing the Moment

Let's look at Bond's encounter with Solange in Casino Royale (you can see the clip here: https://bit.ly/Royale-flirting).

After his high-stakes poker game with an adversary named Dimitrios, Bond wins Dimitrios' Aston Martin. He goes to pick the car up from the valet when Dimitrios wife approaches, not realizing that her husband has lost the car in the bet.

As she sees Bond getting into the car, she recognizes her mistake.

Solange: "No wonder he was in such a foul mood. My mistake."

Bond: "Can I give you a lift home?"

Solange: "That would really send him over the edge…I'm afraid I'm not that cruel."

Bond: "Or perhaps you're just out of practice."

Solange: (laughing) "Perhaps."

Bond: "What about a drink at my place?"

Solange: "You have a place? Is it close?"

Bond: "Very."

They share an interested stare for a few moments.

Solange: "One drink."

And just like that, a night of adventure and passion begins.

There's a few things that happen here:

First, Bond recognizes the opportunity. He senses that she has a mix of curiosity and attraction, and he seizes the moment to push things further.

This isn't to say that you should be attempting this with married women (yikes!), but it demonstrates that it's key to be attuned to her state and how she's feeling.

She attempts to dismiss him from the start by saying she's not that cruel, and then she begins walking away. This is where most men would give up and let it go, thinking that it's over. Or they'd plead for her to reconsider. But Bond knows better.

When he drops the line, "Or perhaps you're just out of practice," he passes her test and reels her back in.

Recognizing the opportunity, he goes in for the close by asking if she wants a drink at his place. From there, it's clear that it's "on."

This shows just how key it is to go in for the close when you have the window of opportunity. Had Bond hesitated or second guessed himself, the window would've closed and he would've missed his chance.

I learned very early on that when you have the opportunity, you've got to take it and act decisively. If you can do this confidently and there's attraction there already, women will usually follow your lead.

And finally, with both this and the first example, Bond exhibits the importance of staying observant and responsive to a woman's signals, as well as understanding when to push things slightly while still respecting her boundaries and comfort level. This keeps the interaction exciting and makes it easier to gently guide things forward.

The Laid-Back Allure of Dex from The Tao Of Steve

Based on appearances, Dex may seem like the polar opposite of James Bond. He's no international spy—he's a part-time kindergarten teacher. But he's got a similar essence of the laid-back cool and confidence of James Bond.

He draws his flirting "game" from the Tao Te Ching and iconic figures like Steve McQueen. **His philosophy revolves around three principles:**

1. Be Desireless: This is all about being nonchalant and indifferent to the outcomes of your interactions with women. Instead of trying too hard to impress or seeking validation, he exudes an aura of self-assuredness and detachment.

2. Be Excellent: His second principal shows the importance of personal excellence and self-improvement. He doesn't need to brag, but he might casually mention a cool project he's working on or a captivating story from his travels, demonstrating his passion and ambition.

3. Be Gone: This is all about knowing when to exit gracefully. He understands that lingering too long or being too clingy can ruin the allure. He gets that it's better to leave the woman wanting more.

This is surprisingly sound dating advice from a Hollywood movie. Being detached from the outcome, pushing toward personal excellence, leaving her wanting more, and avoiding neediness are all common traits of men who succeed with women.

A great example comes early on in the movie when Dex flirts with the bartender at a party (clip here: https://bit.ly/tao-of-steve-flirting).

When ordering a drink, Dex discovers that she's a college student studying philosophy and religion—and also that she doesn't know how to make a Long Island iced tea.

He starts by showing genuine interest in her field of study and then asks a few thought-provoking questions about her philosophical views, listening attentively to her responses. Then, to keep the mood light and fun, he shifts toward playful banter and teases her in a friendly way, showing her how to make a Long Island iced tea through the lens of philosophy and religion.

"A Long Island iced tea is like a survey course in world religions. We're starting with the Far East—you've got Hinduism, Taoism… (as he pours Vodka and then names a few more) …you've got Zoroastrianism… Did you know that Zoroastrians considered dogs the equal of men?"

"I know I do," the bartender replies.

"Good answer," Dex says.

This is where most guys usually go off the rails. They get on a serious subject early on and stick with it, never adding any fun to the interaction. It's a nice conversation, but nothing more than that, and it stays platonic. You need to engage more than her intellectual side if you want to attract her.

But Dex isn't done yet. The bartender is clearly engaged through all of this, and when Dex finishes, she laughs and asks, "So, uh, does this type of thing usually work on young philosophy students?"

Again, most guys would crash and burn here and say something like, "Oh, no—I didn't mean it like that!" or "Sorry I wasn't trying to offend you!"

Instead, Dex stays cool and adds the cherry on top of a quick flirting masterclass: "I don't know. Did it work on you?"

She laughs, and Dex perfectly passes the test.

The Charm of Jacob in Crazy, Stupid, Love

In this movie, Jacob (played by Ryan Gosling) is the epitome of the confident and suave ladies' man.

He's got the look—his style is on point, he's in shape, and totally looksmaxxed—and he's also got the communication skills to back it up.

He hits the same bar throughout the movie and effortlessly picks up women by using his famous line, "You wanna get out of here?" to bring them back to his place.

But the most iconic scene—and also the one from which you can learn the most about flirting with and approaching women—is when he attempts to pick up

Hannah (played by Emma Stone; have a look at the clip here: https://bit.ly/Gosling-flirting).

Jacob struts up to Hannah and her friend mid-conversation, and he breaks in with an observational opener. They're talking about Conan O'Brien and how they think he looks like a carrot.

"Who looks like a carrot?"

This is a perfect observational opener. It assumes familiarity, as it allows him to seamlessly transition into the conversation. It also engages both Hannah and her friend, and he keeps them engaged and acknowledges them both throughout the conversation.

This is a key thing guys screw up when flirting and talking to groups of women. They only talk to the girl they're interested in and ignore the rest of the group. Eventually, the other girls in the group get annoyed and drag their friend away. But because Jacob keeps the friend engaged, she's on his side the whole time.

"We're talking about Conan O'Brien," Hannah's friend replies. "My friend Hannah here thinks he's sexy."

"That's weird, because I think your friend Hannah here is really sexy," Jacob replies.

It's forward, but it comes across as very confident. "Oh my God—you did *not* just say that," Hannah replies, jokingly surprised. There's the first test.

"What are you, a lawyer?" he quips back. There's a quick pattern interrupt—he doesn't answer her question literally and appears unfazed.

And as it turns out, she *is* studying to be a lawyer.

"Aren't you a little old to be using cheesy pick-up lines?" Hannah replies.

"Objection, Your Honor. Leading the witness," Jacob says, playing up on her law background.

Then he breaks into a quick roleplay, as he pretends to be the defense attorney and Hannah is the judge. This allows them to let loose and have fun with each other, and the courtroom setting provides a structured framework for their banter.

He does stumble a little bit unnecessarily from here, saying that he noticed her a couple of hours earlier and thinks that she's beautiful. This isn't needed for where he is in the interaction. Then he tries to push it further while she's testing him—when he hasn't fully passed the tests—which is a bad idea. And asking if she finds him attractive comes across a tad needy; I wouldn't recommend doing that in your interactions.

But then he gets back on track with the courtroom roleplay and saves it a bit. He tells a good story about seizing the day and living in the moment, which is great—you want a woman feeling adventurous around you, as she'll be more apt to go on adventures with you. But this is the wrong context to do it in. If you're going to attempt this, it should be framed as a story that naturally comes up in conversation rather than as an argument trying to convince her to be adventurous. He also comes off a tad too pushy by repeatedly asking her for a drink when she's given him very little buy-in up to that point.

It ends with Hannah rejecting him, at least this time, but he's laid a solid enough foundation and created a memorable experience in her mind. She'll return later and he eventually *does* take that next step with her.

So, there are some good and bad things there—both wise to be aware of. And it's worth noting, too, that not every interaction you have will be perfect. You'll make mistakes, and if your communication fundamentals are on point, women will often be forgiving. But if you make too many in a row or in a short period of time, it can blow up in your face. You want that perfect balance of assuredness and awareness.

Key Takeaways

- **Observation and Adaptability:** James Bond's ability to observe social cues and adapt his flirting style accordingly is a crucial lesson. Being attuned to her signals allows for a more dynamic and engaging interaction, and it allows you to tweak your flirting style to match her personality.

- **Seize the Moment:** Bond's readiness to recognize opportunities and take decisive action highlights why confidence and initiative are key in flirting. Waiting for the perfect moment may mean missing out on potential connections, and once the attraction window closes, it's over. If you don't act fast, you risk missing your chance.

- **Playful Banter and Wit:** Dex from The Tao of Steve and Jacob from Crazy, Stupid, Love showcase the power of witty banter while flirting. Keeping the conversation light-hearted and fun can create a strong rapport and make interactions more memorable.

- **Balance Confidence with Respect:** Confidence is key, but it's also important to be aware of and respect her boundaries. James Bond's assertiveness is tempered with respect for Solange's comfort level, and he guides things forward according to that measure.

Part 2: The Flirting Fundamentals

Where To Meet Women

At this point, you've got a deeper understanding of how to flirt, and we'll continue building on that throughout the rest of the book. But before you can use these skills, you (of course) need to know where to meet women!

Lots of guys struggle with this, especially in the years since COVID—more people are working from home and getting out of the house less on a day-to-day basis.

But with a little intention and an open mind, it's surprisingly easy to meet women in your daily routine, as well as on a casual night out.

And keep in mind that the point isn't to pigeonhole yourself into just one of these ways. You might crush it with online dating, but then things dry up for a few weeks or a month. If you can't approach women in person, you'll be stuck.

But if you've got the power to meet women anywhere, any time, and with any method, your well will never run dry. You'll have plenty of opportunities to create dating abundance so that you can find the right partner.

In this chapter, we'll examine where to meet women during the day, at night, and online.

During the Day

Remember—every time you leave your door, you should see it as an adventure. When you have this mindset, you'll have the openness needed to seize opportunities when they come your way.

Gyms & Fitness Classes

"You can't approach a girl at the gym, bro! She's busy working out!" A TikTok video of mine went viral a few years ago to the tune of millions of views, and it was about how to approach women at the gym.

I had no idea how controversial this subject was, for both men *and* women. Some are vehemently against it while some others are totally for it.

But everything I teach, coach, and talk about is based on experience, not theory. This is something I've tested myself, as well as with thousands of clients over the years. And from that experience, I can say that women are totally open to being talked to at the gym if you do it right (and, of course, respectfully).

Also, it's great for meeting quality women who take care of themselves and have similar values—after all, if you meet at the gym, you're both into self-care and working out.

The keys to talking to women respectfully at the gym:

- Only approach women when they're between sets or entering/leaving the gym.
- Have one or two casual conversations over a week or two before you ask her out so that you can gauge her interest. If she doesn't seem engaged, don't bother asking her out—just keep it friendly.
- Talk to guys at the gym, too. It's a great place to make male friends, and you also won't seem like "that guy" who only talks to all the women.

When it comes to workout classes like yoga, you can have some quick casual conversations before and after class.

Grocery Stores

These are perfect spots for meeting women. Grocery stores are casual environments where people have their guard down and it's easy to strike up conversations. Plus, there's plenty of conversation fodder—there's something new for every aisle, and you can also tease her about what's in her shopping cart. There's really no lack of observational conversation starters.

For example, let's say that you're standing by the avocados. You could ask, "Hey, do you know how to find the perfect ripe avocado? I can never tell if it's just right!"

Another bonus when it comes to grocery stores is that usually people aren't in a rush there, and so it's a relaxed environment where women will generally have a little bit of time to talk.

Parks

This applies to both dog parks and regular parks.

In a regular park, you might find women casually strolling through or even perched up somewhere with a book in hand or with headphones in.

These are all perfect opportunities to start a conversation. If she's wearing headphones, you can ask for playlist recommendations. If she's reading a book, you can make a comment about that. Easy stuff.

Here's a viral video of me approaching a girl at a park in Berlin, Germany: (https://bit.ly/park-approach)

it'll give you a little extra context and motivation to approach the next girl you see in your own park!

And as far as dog parks go, you can make a comment or ask a question about her dog to get the conversation started. Or, if you get lucky, maybe your dog goes and plays with her dog and does some of the leg work for you!

The Mall

Malls in America aren't as good as they used to be for meeting women, but they're still okay choices with plenty of foot traffic going through them. You'll definitely have at least some opportunities.

Malls outside of the USA, however, like in Latin America or Asia, are bustling more than ever before. It seems like a new mall pops up every month in Bangkok, and somehow, it's always crowded. So, if you're living in (or visiting!) a place where mall culture is still huge, definitely take advantage.

Otherwise, you can simply add malls to your toolbox and break them out when some of these other places aren't available, like perhaps in the wintertime.

Busy Downtown Areas

If you live in a big city, you'll want to frequent its bustling urban centers. Peak hours are typically weekend afternoons and early evenings, and also weekday early evenings when everyone gets out of work.

This is where I earned my stripes in the early days of my dating journey, as I met many women near Boylston and Newberry streets in downtown Boston.

These types of areas have high foot traffic, though you'll tend to see more women in a rush than in some of the other locations. That's because they're all usually making their way to and from work, so be cognizant of that. Aim to talk to girls that don't look like they're speeding down the sidewalk.

Boardwalks & The Beach

If you can swing it, these are some of my favorite places to meet women. Of course, not every city or state offers them, but take advantage if they're available to you.

Boardwalks and beaches offer a super relaxed atmosphere and a scenic view, and people are a lot more chilled out than they might be in a downtown type of setting. Plus, women at the beach and on the boardwalk typically have some time on their hands, and it can be an easy place for an "instant date" where you can transition an initial conversation to a full-on date right then and there.

This was one of my favorite things about living in Playa Del Carmen, Mexico. It has a boardwalk type of atmosphere (called La Quinta) right alongside a beautiful beach.

My logistics were set up well—I lived only one street away from the beach. This made it easy to approach girls there, and I had a place to take them back to if things escalated to the next level.

The other nice part about the beach is that women are often on vacation and feeling a tad more adventurous. When she's got a carpe diem attitude, she tends to be open to getting intimate a little more quickly if that's what you're looking to do.

Coffee Shops & Lunch Spots

This is perfect for you guys who work from home. Instead of working from your house every single day, take your laptop to a coffee shop with a great vibe. Sit down in the vicinity of a cute girl and ask her for the Wi-Fi password or what she recommends on the menu. You've already got a few easy conversation starters built into the place. And if your job doesn't allow you to work from home, you can pop into coffee shops in your free time or just go out and grab lunch somewhere cool and popular.

Back when I lived in Bogota, I often met up with my friend at a salad spot for a quick bite to eat in between work sessions.

On one occasion, we saw a group of two cute Colombian women in the corner enjoying a meal. My friend went up and talked to them first, and then I joined in a minute later. They were happy to talk to us, and I ended up taking my girl out on several dates and enjoying a great time with her around Colombia. And all it took was a quick, two-minute conversation with her before I returned to the table to eat with my friend. Don't let opportunities like these slip!

The Farmer's Market

When it comes to meeting women, farmer's markets are like grocery stores on steroids. You've got all the good things about grocery stores but mixed with an open-air environment, more of a chill atmosphere, and even more health-focused women.

If you've got one of these in your area, you should definitely check it out. And it's an easy opportunity to see if she has similar eating habits and values, too.

For example, I like to eat a lot of meat, so I know if she's at the grass-fed meat stand or lined up at the raw milk dairy stand, we'll probably get along well!

Bookstores & Libraries

It's hard to believe sometimes, but bookstores and libraries are still alive and kicking. They may not be as popular as in decades past, but you can absolutely still meet women there.

These places offer a quiet and comfortable environment, easy for starting a conversation in. They're usually not too crowded either, and so you don't need to worry about too many people eavesdropping on your conversation. Plus, there's lots of conversation fodder here—everything from the book aisle she's into the book she's reading.

At Night

"I'm not a partier, man. I don't like to meet women at night." "There are no quality girls out at night!"

"No, I don't drink, so I can't go out."

I've heard these things *a million* times. And I get it—nightlife has a reputation for lower-quality women and a lot of drinking.

But to be honest, these aren't good excuses to completely avoid these environments.

First, who says that you need to drink when you go out? You can have plenty of fun sober. Second, you don't need to go to a huge techno club every time you go out. You can go to more chill places—places where there's actually a higher volume of quality women.

And, again, I say this based on my experience from coaching many guys in different environments, as well as meeting my own girlfriends in different ways—during the day, at night, and online (which we'll get to in a bit).

What's unique about nightlife is that it gives you the highest volume of attractive women in a small vicinity. You can't get that anywhere else, not even in really high foot-traffic places. Even if only for getting tons of practice in a short amount of time, it's worth exploring what some nightlife has to offer.

Now as far as where to go, let's look at some options.

Upscale Bars & Lounges

These are far and away my go-to choice when it comes to nightlife. This is where you'll find high-quality, classy women, and the music isn't blaring so it's easy to start and maintain a conversation.

Most women who go to these environments are open to chatting—and they're usually in smaller groups which makes it even easier to approach them. Plus, people aren't usually getting plastered drunk like they typically do at big clubs, and there's less stimulation. It's easy to get a woman's attention squarely focused on you at these places.

If you can find it, the perfect mix is an upscale lounge that has a small dance floor or dance room. This allows you to get the best of both worlds.

Other Nightlife

Dive Bars

These are more cozy, unpretentious kinds of venues. They're certainly not high end, but they offer relaxing atmospheres where it's very easy to get conversations going.

I recommend checking these out during the week. You can pop in and get a game of billiards going with friends, and if you see a cute girl, you can go say hi.

Concerts & Live Music Venues/Music Festivals

These atmospheres aren't the most ideal for making long-term connections. Most people go in big groups, there's a lot of stimulation, and if you hit it off with a girl, you can't easily leave to somewhere more intimate, at least not for a few hours until the show is over.

However, they can be great for chatting up a bunch of people, making new friends, and getting some practice in. These are more for the experience of having fun, and any girls you meet along the way are a nice bonus.

Big Nightclubs

These also have a lot of stimulation and lots of big groups. That said, you can get plenty of conversations going, and you can bring girls to the dance floor as well, which makes it a little easier to escalate things.

Big nightclubs present more of a fast-paced game, though. You've got to be well-versed in the flirting techniques we'll dive into, especially push-pull and leading/dominance—otherwise you won't be able to keep women engaged over the course of the night.

Online

Meeting women online used to be fairly taboo about 15 years ago, but times have definitely changed. These days, if you're not meeting women online, you're playing the game with a serious handicap. Later on, we'll dive into how to flirt online, but for now let's take a look at the best ways to get started on bringing your internet dating game well up to par.

The Best Dating Apps

This depends a bit on where you're located. If you're in Europe or Latin America, for example, Tinder and Bumble are the most popular dating apps, but Hinge is gaining traction.

In the USA, Hinge is one of the more premium dating apps, while Bumble is decently second tier, and Tinder tends to be the most spammy, catering to a younger crowd and filled with plenty of bots and fake profiles.

Here's a quick look at each of the most popular dating apps:

- **Hinge** brands itself as more of a relationship-focused app, and the women on there tend to be looking for relationships more than anything else (although plenty are open to short-term flings). As I mentioned, it's one of the more premium dating apps—and it's also my #1 choice for the USA.

- **Bumble** is the go-to in Latin America but also widely used throughout the USA and Europe. The unique spin with Bumble is that only women can start the conversation after you match.

- **Tinder** is the most well-known dating app and the most popular one globally. It's more hookup-oriented and it tends to be a little bit lower quality, although you can still meet some awesome women on it.

- **The League** is more of a premium dating app, focusing on young professional "high achievers." But you need to pass a bit of a rigorous screening process to get onto it, and so there's a lower volume of people. That said, there's definitely some quality women on there.

- **Raya** is similar to The League in that it requires users to apply for membership, and you're vetted based on different criteria. It's been known as the "celebrity dating app," as a lot of higher profile people are on it.

Honestly, I'd recommend starting with Hinge, Tinder, and Bumble. Put some effort into taking high-quality photos; don't just take random shots of your life.

You really need to intentionally go out and take photos specifically for this—and if you can afford professional shots, that's the most ideal. If not, you can use portrait mode on your camera phone.

For pose, style, and background inspiration, check out our Beast Photos Instagram at www.instagram.com/beastphotos_official/. These are the kinds of photos that are considered "top quality" and will get you plenty of matches and dates.

The Power of Instagram

Even though it's not technically a dating app, Instagram is, in many ways, the best dating app at this point. It allows you to connect with women from all over the world, brand yourself as a high-quality guy, and solidify your interactions from dating apps and in-person conversations. Let's say that you're talking to a girl for two minutes, make a pretty good impression, and then close the conversation by getting her Instagram.

She doesn't have a ton to remember you by in the conversation, but when she takes a look at your Instagram profile later, she's blown away. You've got premium-looking photos, high-quality story highlights, and overall, it's clear that you know how to represent yourself well. She's going to be far more likely to want to follow through and hang out with you in this case, rather than if you had a bunch of awkward selfies and low-quality photos like most guys do.

Aside from building up your communication and flirting abilities, optimizing your Instagram and dating apps with great photos is the highest-leverage thing you can do. It can assert yourself as a top 5 to 10% man that women compete over, and it'll make all the strategies you'll discover in this book work even better.

Diving into the ins and outs of optimizing your Instagram is a bit out of the scope of this book, **but you can listen to me dive in-depth into it in this podcast episode:** https://spoti.fi/4389qP2.

Key Takeaways

- **Diversify Your Approach:** Don't rely solely on one method to meet women. Keep your options open and be adaptable to different environments and situations.

- **Daytime Opportunities:** Capitalize on everyday scenarios like the gym, grocery store, parks, malls, and downtown areas. These settings offer relaxed atmospheres conducive to starting conversations.

- **Nightlife Exploration:** While not everyone's jam, nightlife venues provide opportunities to meet a high volume of women in a small vicinity. Approach with an open mind and consider more intimate, low-key settings, and keep the drinking to a minimum (or just cut it out completely) so that you can stay socially sharp.

- **Online Dating:** Embrace the shift toward online dating platforms like Hinge, Bumble, and Tinder. Put effort into creating high-quality profiles with intentional photos to match with and date higher-quality women.

- **Instagram's Influence:** Leverage Instagram as a powerful dating tool. Optimize your profile with premium photos to stand out to top-tier women from both online and in-person conversations.

What Good Flirting Looks Like

"I'm pretty good at talking to people, but women always tell me that they don't feel a connection. I don't get it!"

This is a really common thing I hear from guys who struggle with women. They often think that their dates and conversations are going well, but for some reason, women never seem to feel the same attraction.

Here's the thing: "Talking to people" at your work, within a friendship, or in your day-to-day life is *completely* different than flirting with a woman on a more seductive level. You can absolutely be amazing at the former and terrible at the latter.

And if you struggle to get girls out on dates, get past the first date, or move things forward with women in general, there's a good chance that your flirting ability (or lack thereof) is the culprit.

But once you fix that, you'll be able to spike a woman's attraction quite quickly and solve a lot of those mishaps.

The first step to fixing it is to understand what good flirting actually looks like, so let's dive in.

It's Subtle Instead of Blunt

Flirting has a finesse to it. Think of it like leaving breadcrumbs instead of drawing a treasure map. Good flirting brings her into your world, but it also adds a little mystery and charm that's hard to resist. You don't let on that she fully has you—not just yet.

When you have the ability and patience to give her a sneak preview instead of the whole movie, it's powerful and it keeps her wanting more.

Here's some great ways to be subtle with your flirting. **You can use:**

- Body language cues. Maintain eye contact, smile warmly, lean in to convey your interest, and then back out to keep her wanting more.
- Innuendos. These can be a great way to imply something on the spicier side without outright saying it.
- Suggestive questions and assumptions to get her to open up.
    - For example, "You seem like the adventurous type."

It's Playful Instead of Overly Serious

Flirting is also playful. This is a hard thing to grasp for many guys who take themselves so seriously in different aspects of life. But hey—this is *not* the time to be uptight.

Let's say that there's a woman in line in front of you at the coffee shop. Instead of diving straight into compliments about how beautiful she is, you have a playful exchange that keeps the mood light and intriguing.

"Decisions, decisions," you say with a grin as you nod toward the menu board.

She looks over and smiles, and you continue.

"I've been staring at the menu for a few minutes myself. Let me guess—you're more of a cappuccino girl, but you're feeling a little adventurous today?"

"How'd you know?" she laughs. "I might finally go for that pumpkin spice latte."

You raise an eyebrow playfully. "Stepping out of your comfort zone, huh? I like it," you say with a grin, appreciating her spontaneity. You've just turned a mundane conversation about coffee into a fun and playful one. And now it's easy to bridge the conversation from here into a new topic.

A simple exercise to be more playful in conversation is simply to think, "How can I make this a little more fun?" The goal isn't to be a Jack Black-style goofball—it's to add a little flavor into your conversations.

It's Self-Assured Instead of Insecure

When you're confident in yourself and your intentions, you don't second guess every move you make while flirting. You know what you want and you're comfortable expressing it—whether it's showing interest, making a playful remark, or asking her out. This confidence allows you to flirt authentically without fear of rejection or judgment.

To be good at flirting, you need to do it from a place of self-amusement and genuine enjoyment—not because you're seeking validation or approval from the woman. You're not overly concerned with how she'll perceive it. If she vibes with your flirting style, great. If not, it might not be a good fit anyway (or you might just need to work a little more on your flirting ability).

This allows you to detach from the outcome, which leaves room to be more authentic, genuine, and fully present in the moment.

It provides a stark contrast with the men who are totally focused on trying to impress her, which usually comes off quite cringey. And you definitely don't want to be that guy.

It Adds to the Connection

Flirting doesn't just add banter and fun to the interaction—it also adds to the connection.

You engage with her emotionally, and there's an element of vulnerability there as you both reveal different aspects about yourselves, your interests, and your senses of humor. Plus, it gives you the chance to develop inside jokes and playful gestures, as well as explore shared interests.

In essence, you bring her into your world for a few moments.

For example, let's say that you're on a date with a girl and it goes something like this:

You: (playfully nudging her arm) "So Kate, tell me—what's your secret talent? I bet you're hiding something impressive."

Kate: (laughs) "Hmm, well, I make a killer chocolate chip cookie. Does that count?"

You: (grinning) "Absolutely! Now, the *real* question is—when do I get to taste these legendary cookies?"

Kate: (teasingly) "Ah, that's the million-dollar question, isn't it? Maybe if you're lucky, I'll cook them for you one day."

You: "Consider me intrigued. Looks like I'll have to stick around to uncover the mystery. Just don't hate me if I unleash my inner Gordon Ramsey on your cookies."

You and Kate have some playful banter back and forth, and you're able to turn what could've been a potentially bland conversation about cookies into a flirty exchange that creates a sense of connection and mutual interest. Also, it hints at seeing each other again in the future.

It's Risky...But Not Too Risky

Most guys are afraid to take risks in their conversations. Instead of seizing the opportunity to say something edgy or fun, they filter themselves and end up boring the girl. This usually results in an interview-mode conversation that leads nowhere.

"Where are you from?"

"How many brothers or sisters do you have?"

"What are your plans this weekend?"

If all you focus on is questions like these and never try to build off them to make things fun, your conversations will fall flat. Remember—it's okay to cross the line occasionally with something you say; this shows you where the line is! It also shows confidence.

And all good flirting comes with risk.

It involves putting yourself (and your humor) out there and being vulnerable. When you're expressing interest, making jokes, and adding in some physical touch, there's always a risk of misinterpretation or rejection, but you'll rarely get anywhere without taking those chances.

It also involves testing boundaries, whether through playful teasing or suggestive comments. This can create excitement and build attraction, but it also carries the risk of making her uncomfortable if not done tactfully.

However, all this comes with the territory, right? To be good at flirting, you *must* embrace the risk of it. After all, all good things lie on the other side of a good risk, so it's always better to be bold.

That being said, you don't need to take it all the way to the extreme. **You can take calculated risks while flirting, and here's how:**

- Read the room. Pay attention to her body language and verbal cues to gauge her interest and comfort level. If she seems receptive, you can gradually escalate things, and if she seems disinterested, you can dial it back.

- Start small. Begin with light-hearted banter and subtle compliments before diving into suggestive or intimate topics.

- Be genuine. Authenticity is key to successful flirting. Use flirting as a tool to express yourself and bring her in on the fun.

Key Takeaways

- **Flirting Is Different from Regular Conversation:** Being good at chatting with friends doesn't automatically translate to successful flirting with women. Recognize that flirting involves a different dynamic and set of techniques.

- **Subtle and Playful:** Effective flirting is subtle rather than blunt. Inject playfulness into your interactions to keep the mood light and engaging. This can turn mundane conversations into enjoyable exchanges that build rapport.

- **Self-Assurance Is Key:** Confidence is attractive. Be comfortable expressing your intentions and interests without seeking validation from the woman. Detach from the outcome and focus on enjoying the interaction for what it is.

- **Deepen the Connection:** Good flirting goes beyond surface-level banter. It adds depth to the interaction by engaging with the woman emotionally and revealing shared interests and humor. Use it as a tool to bring her into your world and create a sense of connection and mutual interest.

- **Embrace Calculated Risks:** Flirting involves some level of risk. Start with small, light-hearted gestures and gradually escalate based on her interest level. Be genuine and authentic in your approach, and also be willing to take bold but calculated risks to build attraction.

By the way, do you want some extra help putting all these new flirting strategies into action?

I created the **Dating Mastery Bundle** to provide you with just that. In it, you'll get the following bonuses:

- The First Date Playbook
- Get a Girlfriend in 30 Days – Audio Guide
- 5 Texting Mistakes that Destroy Attraction – Audio Guide
- The Approach Anxiety Buster PDF
- The Top-Tier Dating Profile Kickstart

To get instant access, go to **daveperrotta.com/mastery.**

The Irresistible Flirting Techniques of Top 5% Men

You've now got a much deeper understanding of flirting and what attracts women, which means that you're equipped with a solid base.

Now let's examine some actual techniques that you can roll out in your conversations.

Tonality

When it comes to flirting, it's not just about what you say—it's also about how you say it. Your tonality refers to your voice and overall manner of speaking, as well as how that adds (or subtracts) from the charm and effectiveness of your flirting.

Specifically, I'm referring to your pitch, pace, volume, inflection, expression, pausing, and emphasis. Let's flesh out how to get all these down the right way—otherwise, the rest of the techniques we'll cover will fall completely flat.

Key Elements of Effective Tonality

1. Speaking Slowly

Talking at a slower pace adds a sense of deliberation and confidence to your words. It allows her to absorb what you're saying, creating a sense of intimacy and significance.

Most guys talk about two to three times faster than they should when communicating with women. As a general rule, you should slow it down until you feel like it's a little *too* slow. It may seem a bit weird at first, but that's probably the right pace!

2. Low-Pitched Tone

Women *love* men with deeper voices. A lower tone of voice conveys a sense of calm and confidence. Avoiding uptalk, which is when your voice rises at the end of sentences, is crucial. Keeping your tone even or slightly downward at the end of sentences makes you seem more certain.

Below are a few tips to speak with a lower-pitched voice:

- **Relax Your Throat:** When your throat is tense, it can actually constrict your voice and make it higher. Try to relax your throat muscles, as this leads to a deeper, fuller sound.
- **Breath Control:** Breathe deeply from your diaphragm (the muscle just below your rib cage) rather than your chest. This type of breathing supports a stronger and deeper voice.
- **Lower Your Pitch Gradually:** Start speaking at your natural pitch, and then gradually lower it to a comfortable level. Avoid straining your voice—the goal here is to sound deeper while still sounding natural.
- **Mindful Speaking:** Be aware of your voice during conversations. If you notice your pitch rising due to excitement or nerves, take a moment to pause and re-adjust.

- **Record and Listen:** Recording your voice and listening back can provide insight into your natural tone and areas for improvement. I have my clients do this all the time so that we can point out and adjust the weak points of their tonality.

- **Voice Exercises:** Try these to strengthen your vocal cords.
    - **For example**, you can hum at different pitches, starting higher and then going lower, to find your natural deep tone.

3. Facial Expressions & The Seductive Smile

Your facial expressions should complement your tonality. A genuine, warm smile or a subtle, playful smirk can make your words more powerful.

You can also break out the "seductive smile"—this is a subtle, knowing smile, with minimal teeth showing and a light squint. Ryan Gosling's character Jacob in Crazy, Stupid, Love often uses this technique, so check some clips to get an idea.

4. Relaxed & Playful Attitude

You want to convey a laid-back, easygoing attitude through your voice, as it makes the conversation feel light and enjoyable. It also shows you're comfortable and enjoying the interaction, which makes her more relaxed, too.

5. Matching Energy Levels

Part of effective tonality is adapting to the energy of the conversation. If she's speaking with excitement, slightly increase your energy level to match hers. In more intimate or serious moments, a softer, lower tone can create a sense of closeness.

6. The Power of Pauses

Well-timed pauses can add emphasis to your words, create suspense, or give space for her to add to the conversation. They make you sound more interesting and your words seem more captivating.

One of my favorite ways to use pauses is on the approach.

For example, "Hey…I know this is super, super random…but I saw you…and I thought you were stunning…and I had to meet you for a minute…I'm Dave." These pauses in between certain parts of what you're saying to her can be irresistible and leave her hanging on your words.

7. Volume Control

Adjust your volume to suit the environment. In quieter settings, use a softer, more inviting tone. In louder settings, speak clearly and loudly to make sure that she hears you.

Practical Application in Flirting Scenarios

- During a date, if she shares something personal with you, respond with a softer, empathetic tone and a gentle smile to show understanding and interest.

- When using playful banter, use a slightly quicker pace and a more animated tone, paired with expressive facial gestures, to keep the energy lively.

- When giving a compliment or asking a flirty question, slow down and lower your pitch slightly to add sincerity and depth to your words.

Teasing

Teasing is when you make fun of a girl in a playful manner. It's basically a mix of witty banter that adds a little twist to the conversation, all while keeping it respectful and light. You never insult her—it's more like poking innocent fun.

Let's look at a few examples of teasing in action below.

Her: "I'm really into astrology."

Good tease: "Oh, wow—you're totally a libra, aren't you? This is never gonna work."

Bad tease: "You believe in that stuff? Sounds pretty superstitious to me."

Her: "I love to cook. "

Good tease: "Oh, a chef, huh? So, when you say 'cooking,' are we talking gourmet meals or expert-level grilled cheese?"

Bad tease: "I knew it—you belong in the kitchen."

Her: "I love Game of Thrones."

Good tease: "Yeah, I'm kinda getting Cersei vibes from you, actually."

Bad tease: "Wow, you're such a nerd, aren't you?"

Here's how you can tease effectively:

- **Read Her Responses:** How does she react to your teasing? If she laughs or teases back, it's a good sign. If she shuts down or seems uncomfortable, it's time to pull back.

- **Keep It Light:** Teasing should be light and respectful. Avoid sensitive topics like religion, politics, appearance, style, or personal issues.

- **Back-and-Forth Banter:** Teasing is a two-way street—you both should be getting in on the fun. This creates a fun and playful interaction, and it shows that you can dish it out as well as you can take it.

- **Don't Self-Deprecate:** Do this too often, and you'll come off like you lack confidence.

- **Make sure that your tonality is on point:** Smile when you tease, use a light tone, and make sure it's clear that you're being playful.

- **Don't Lay It on Too Thick:** Sometimes guys get carried away and tease her too much. Keep a balance between teasing, other flirting styles, and actually getting to know her.

Passing Her Tests

Women—especially quality women—are going to test you often, especially early on in the dating process. She tests you because she wants to see that you are who you say you are. Can you hold up against a little pushback, or do you fold at the first sign of pressure?

When she tests you, it's actually a *good* thing. She's rooting for you to pass and to give her a reason to be more interested. And then it's on you where to take it.

One of the best ways to pass her tests is to agree and exaggerate. This is when you take what she says, amplify it humorously, and show her that you're not easily fazed. It keeps the conversation fun and playful rather than turning it into a serious discussion (and you failing the test).

Another good way is to put it back on her. This is where you playfully turn the statement back in her direction, create a playful back-and-forth dynamic, and essentially give her the same test.

Let's look at a few examples of this in action:

Her: "Just so you know, I don't sleep with guys on the first date."

Exaggerate: "Thank God, because I'm saving myself for marriage."

Back on her: "You're getting a little ahead of yourself here. You need to wine and dine me first."

Bad: "Don't worry! I'd never try that tonight."

Her: "I normally don't date guys your age."

Exaggerate: "Fair enough. I'm actually 85 at heart. I just work out a lot and have an exceptional skincare routine."

Back on her: "That's okay. I'll slow down a little so that you can keep up."

Bad: "Age is just a number. It's not a big deal!"

Her: "You probably say that to every girl."

Exaggerate: "Of course. I've got it scripted and everything. You're right at the point where you're charmed and intrigued."

Back on her: "Right, and you're the mysterious one who's heard it all before. Quite the dynamic we have here."

Bad: "I don't say this to other girls, I swear!"

Misinterpretation

This is when you playfully misconstrue something she says as an advance or innuendo. Again, you want to keep it light here and slightly suggestive without crossing the line into being vulgar or offensive.

The point is to add a playful spin to the conversation and position yourself as the prize. It can be great as well for getting more "innocent" girls to start showing you their "not-so-innocent" side. And, as with all flirting, subtlety is key.

Below, some examples of misinterpretation:

Her: "Oh my God, I love dancing!"

Good: "You must have good rhythm then, huh? That's important for a lot of things."

Bad: "You must be really good in bed then." (too vulgar)

Her: "I'm really into yoga."

Good: "Yoga, huh? I've always admired flexibility—in *all* aspects of life."

Bad: "Wow, I bet you can bend in some interesting ways." (too suggestive)

Her: (early on in a date) "I actually live across the street from here."

Good: "Wow, slow down! At least buy me a drink before you invite me over."

Bad: "Let's go there right now." (too forward and fast)

What's good about misinterpretation is that it can give you a sense of where you stand with her. If she plays along or even takes that line of conversation to a further level, there's a solid chance that she has high interest in you. If she's neutral, it's still a good sign because at least she's not shutting it down. But if she *does* shut it down completely, you've got some work to do.

Push/Pull

Push/pull is a flirting technique in which you balance showing interest (the pull) and playfully teasing or feigned disinterest (the push). This creates intrigue, leaves her wanting more, and sparks interest.

Understanding Push/Pull

The pull draws her closer emotionally, often through compliments, expressions of interest, or showing a deeper level of investment. Basically, it signals attraction.

The push, in contrast, creates a playful challenge or barrier, usually through teasing, light-hearted criticism, or playful disinterest. It adds an element of unpredictability to the interaction.

The following are some examples of push/pull in action:

Her: "Really? I hate sushi."

Push: "I can't believe you don't like sushi! This is never going to work."

Her: "Yeah, such a bummer."

Pull: "Well, good thing you're kinda cute. Maybe I can look past the sushi."

Pull: "I really respect that you prioritize your fitness."

Her: "Thank you! I've been going hard lately."

Push: "Let me feel you flex real quick. (hold her bicep area) Okay, you can flex now." (the joke is that you act like you can't tell that she's flexing when she actually is)

You: "Let's go back to my place (pull), but only if you promise not to make any moves on me (push)."

There's also a non-verbal side to push/pull. This is all about body language, and opening and closing the space between the two of you. If you weave this into your interactions the right way, she'll begin to crave your touch and want to get closer to you.

Below are some ways you can push/pull non-verbally:

1. Lean In and Out During the Conversation

Pull: Leaning in during an important or intimate part of the conversation signals interest and creates a moment of closeness. This is easy to do at louder nighttime venues, where you can lean in and talk in her ear for a moment, and then lean back out again.

Push: Leaning out slightly after sharing a moment of laughter or an interesting point in the conversation creates a temporary space between you and makes her miss your touch.

2. Arm Gestures

Push: Casually placing your arm around her for a minute and then naturally pulling away adds a layer of comfort and spontaneity. She knows that you're comfortable doing it without being overbearing.

Pull: The initial act of putting your arm around her is a warm, inviting gesture that can work well when used sparingly.

3. Dance Dynamics

Push: While the two of you are dancing, intentionally creating a little space after a close move adds an element of playfulness. You're not "all up in her grill" for too long that it makes her uncomfortable. You're able to let it breathe.

Pull: Dancing closely, especially during a slow or romantic song, establishes a physical connection and intimacy.

(Note: Reggaeton is *perfect* for this. This style of music makes it easy to dance close, back away, then come back in close again. And actually, Latin dancing in general makes this quite easy if you have a little rhythm.

4. Tease the Kiss

Push: Lean in as if thinking of kissing her and building anticipation, but then gently pull back, prolonging the moment and increasing her desire. She *knows* that you know that you can get it, and you both know that you're going to do it—you're just playfully making her wait for it.

Pull: The initial lean-in, paired with slow talking and eye contact, creates a magnetic pull that draws her into the moment.

You can also do this with an actual kiss, but this is actually where many guys screw up. Once they get a kiss, they go for a full-on, ten-minute makeout. You might think that this is a win but it kills *all* the tension—especially after what may have been a solid first date.

There's a time and a place for long makeouts—generally when you're somewhere private where intimacy is possible. Otherwise, it over-validates her, creates too much "pull," and actually makes her less excited to see you again (and yes—if this sounds familiar, the long makeout session by your car may have been why you didn't get that second date).

What's far better is to use push/pull with the actual kiss—kiss her for three to five seconds and then be the first one to pull back. You can do this several times throughout the interaction. It's never enough to fully validate her, but just enough to spike the tension and leave her wanting more.

Then, once you're eventually back in private, the built-up tension can lead to a passionate night.

5. Playful Touches

Push: Lightly touch her arm or shoulder during the flow of conversation and then pull your hand back. You can also put your hand on her leg or around her waist for a few moments before pulling it back. This makes her comfortable with your touch and gets her craving more of it.

Pull: Initiating these light touches expresses interest and creates a connection.

6. Eye Contact Dynamics

Push: Breaking eye contact after a shared laugh or a moment of connection leaves her wanting more.

Pull: Holding eye contact during key parts of the conversation indicates deep interest and connection.

Here's the best way to think about flirty eye contact: As you look into her eyes, you have the mindset of, "This is fun, and I know you're into it," and also, "You're cute, but let's see what else you've got."

It's like a playful little game of cat and mouse. You both understand what's going on—and you're both enjoying it.

7. Adjusting Space

Push: Occasionally adjusting your position to create a bit of distance can build intrigue and make her more inclined to close the gap.

Pull: Closing the space, like when moving in to share something private, creates a sense of exclusivity and intimacy.

Future Projecting

This term describes a flirting technique in which you create fun, fictional scenarios about future adventures or experiences with the person you're flirting with. It's a perfect way to transition from simply having a fun and flirty conversation to creating a sense of possibility and togetherness.

The Art of Future Projecting

Creating Shared Scenarios: These scenarios involve both of you in an imagined future that's enjoyable and exciting. It's a way of subtly suggesting compatibility and shared interests while indicating that this conversation could actually lead somewhere.

Building a Connection: By talking about shared future experiences, you're not only deepening the rapport but also planting seeds for potential future dates or interactions.

When to Use Future Projecting:

- **After Building Rapport:** It's best used once you've established a connection and she's showing interest. Jumping into future projecting too early can come off as presumptuous.
- **Align with Her Interests:** If she mentions a hobby or a dream, like traveling to Asia or learning salsa dancing, use that information to build your scenario.
- **Detail-Oriented:** Adding details helps her to visualize and engage with the scenario more vividly.
- **Inclusive Language:** Use "we" to make it inclusive and create a sense of togetherness.

Below are some examples of future projecting in action:

Traveling Together Scenario:

Her: "I've always wanted to visit Asia."

You: "Me too—imagine us exploring the streets of Tokyo, getting things lost in translation and laughing about it, and finding the best sushi spot in the city. But I have to warn you that I take my karaoke seriously."

Learning a New Skill Together:

Her: "I've always wanted to learn salsa dancing."

You: "We'd crush it on the dance floor. I can picture us now—gracefully out of sync at first, but soon after that, we're the stars of the dancefloor. Just promise that you won't outshine me on the first lesson."

Sharing A Fun Experience Together:

Her: "I've always wanted to try skydiving."

You: "Okay, that's it then—we're going skydiving. You handle the screaming and I'll handle the courage. We'll just freefall and hope for the best. *You're* doing the mid-air backflips, though."

The key with future projecting is to keep it hypothetical. If you try to actually make specific plans, it ruins the fun, creates a weird dynamic, and immediately makes you seem like a guy who "doesn't get it." Basically, you don't want to use the skydiving joke and then say, "Oh, I know this skydiving school we can go to! Does next Saturday work for you?" Instead, you keep her skydiving dreams in mind for a future date and then bring it up later on if you guys continue to hang out.

Flirty Questions

These are fun and easy tools that you can break out to spice up your dates and interactions. They create tension, shift things to a more flirty mood, and give you insights into her preferences and personality.

Setting the Stage for Flirty Questions

- **Timing:** These questions work best once you've built a little rapport—launching into them too early might seem abrupt or uncalibrated.

- **Reading the Room:** Gauge her comfort level and response to your initial conversation. If she seems open and engaged, it's a good sign for you to introduce flirty questions.

Types of Flirty Questions

- **Light and Playful:** These are questions that are fun and easy to answer, which sets a lighthearted mood.

Some examples:

  - "If you could have any superpower for just one day, what would it be…and would you use it to woo me?"
  - "If you could wake up anywhere in the world tomorrow, where would it be?"

- **A Bit Provocative:** These are slightly edgier questions that tread into the territory of flirtation and attraction, and they're designed to build tension.

Some examples:

  - "What's something that always turns your head when you see a guy?"
  - "What do you find sexiest in a guy?"
  - "What was your last crazy adventure?"
  - "What's the worst first date you've ever been on?" (The great thing about this is that it's a loaded question—it assumes that the date she's on with you right now is a good one!)

- **Personal but Intriguing**: These questions allow her to share more about herself in a playful context.

Some examples:

- "What's one thing that I wouldn't guess about you?"
- "What kinds of things make you laugh the hardest?"
- "What did you want to be when you grew up?"

Responding to Her Answers

When it comes to responding, you can mix your genuine thoughts with a bit of fun and playfulness. This can help springboard the conversation into something deeper, and you can weave in and out between light flirting and deeper topics.

For example, let's say you ask her, "What do you find sexiest in a guy?"

Her: "I love when a guy is confident and has a great sense of humor. Lookswise? Dark hair, blue eyes, and a great smile." (And if she likes you, she'll typically describe *you* when she answers this question, which is always awesome!)

You: "Okay, so you like to keep it light and have some fun. I like that—I'm the same way. Can't take yourself too seriously. (smiling) Blue eyes and dark hair though, huh?" (assuming that those things describe you)

Her: (laughs) "Yeah, you caught me. What about you—what do you like in a girl?"

From here, if you like her, you can lightly describe her in return, along with some qualities you'd like her to embody. She'll often start trying to prove that she *has* these qualities.

You: "Well, I like girls with long brown hair and good style...girls who are independent and have a little bit of an adventurous side. You know—girls who don't care what people think all that much."

Her: "Oh, yeah? Well, I guess I have a little bit of an adventurous side..."

You: (smiling) "I'll have to see that for myself..."

Key Takeaways

- **Tonality - The Secret Sauce:** Slow down the pace of your speaking and drop your voice a notch—you'll project confidence with every word. And don't forget that smirk or seductive smile—it adds flavor to what you're saying and helps you convey the right vibe.

- **Teasing - Keep It Fun, Not Insulting:** Tease her like you're in on a private joke together. It's not about taking digs—it's about playful banter that gets her smiling. Watch her reactions; if she's laughing and firing back, you're golden.

- **Passing Her Tests:** When she throws you a curveball, hit it out of the park by agreeing and exaggerating. Show her that her little tests don't faze you. Keep it light, keep it fun, and keep it moving.

- **Master Push/Pull:** Draw her in both physically and verbally with genuine interest, then toss a bit of a challenge her way with a mix of savvy banter and the right body language (like dancing up close, then further away, and repeating).

- **Future Projecting and Planting a Seed of Adventure:** Spin tales about adventures that you could have together. It's not planning—it's fantasizing out loud. These are like "us against the world" scenarios. Make her laugh—and make her wonder, "What if?"

- **Spice Things Up with Flirty Questions:** Once you've got a good rhythm going, pop in some flirty questions. Keep it spicy but not too heavy, and you'll get a sense for how open she is (and how willing she is to play into innuendos and "edgier" topics).

- **Strike the Balance:** All this flirting is great, but don't forget to mix in some real talk, too. It's not just about being the fun guy—he's forgettable. When you're fun *and* real, she won't be able to stop thinking about you.

Part 3: How to Flirt in Key Situations

How to Flirt When You First Meet Her

You see a girl and you want to talk to her. Now what?

This isn't about walking up to her and throwing a pickup line her way. It's about kicking off the interaction with a solid vibe and creating a spark.

Let's talk about how to start this off with a bang and not a fizzle. When it comes to initiating the conversation, you've got a few great options, which we'll explore below.

Situational Openers: Your Environment Is Your Wingman

These openers involve you using your surroundings as a launchpad for the conversation. The nice part about these is that they can feel a little smoother, and they also demonstrate that you can be observant and quick on your feet.

Basically, you're showing her that you're not just another guy with a line—you're someone who can turn an everyday moment into something a bit more exciting. Plus, it's a low-pressure way to gauge her interest. If she bites and plays along, you're in good shape. If not, no big deal—you just keep it moving.

Let's look at a few examples of flirty situational openers:

Grocery Store Gambit

Picture this perfect setup: You're both eyeing the avocados. Roll in with something like, "Ever feel like choosing the right avocado is like defusing a bomb? Pick the wrong one and your guac's a goner." Something like this is effective because it's relatable, everyday stuff but you're making it fun.

Gym Tactics

Maybe she's trying a new machine during her workout. Slide in with, "That machine's a beast, right? I swear it's half workout and half puzzle trying to figure it out."

What's the winning angle here? You're in the same boat, and it's a shared challenge.

Park Play

Maybe you see her at the park and she's reading or jogging. A comment like, "That book any good? I'm on the hunt for my next park bench read" can work wonders. The edge here is that you're showing interest in her taste, and it's a great segue into deeper topics.

The Drink Observation

Let's say she's at the bar trying to decide what to order, or maybe she's just received an unusual-looking drink. Lean in (not too close—mind her personal space) with a hint of a smile and say something like, "That drink looks like it has a story behind it. Is it as good as it looks or are you just being adventurous tonight?"

Non-Situational Openers: Straight Shooting

Sometimes the situation itself doesn't give you much to work with, especially in fast-paced environments like a busy street or a lively festival.

This is where non-situational openers come into play. They're about diving in with either a direct or an indirect approach and cutting through the noise—you're making your intentions clear but in a smooth and calibrated way.

The Direct Approach

A direct opener is straight-forward and leaves no room for ambiguity. It's a clear, confident approach in which you're expressing your interest from the start.

Let's look at some examples:

Compliment-Based: "Excuse me, I just noticed you from across the room and had to say that your sense of style is amazing. I'm (your name)."

Interest Declaration: "Hey, I know this might be random, but I saw you standing here and felt compelled to come over and meet you. I'm (your name)."

What makes the direct opener effective is that it shows confidence and honesty, and it sets the tone for the interaction.

This works best in situations where social interaction isn't expected, like walking down the street, at a park, and in other everyday situations. Not at the gym though—if you use the direct approach there, you'll quickly come across as "that guy" hitting on every girl. Stick to a situational approach in that environment.

That said, direct openers can also work decently well in situations where social interaction is expected, like bars and lounges. Usually they're not as needed there, as you have so much situational fodder to use—but if you spot a total knockout and feel compelled to go direct, go for it.

Nightlife Openers

Let's quickly cover some more openers you can use in nightlife settings when there's a bit more stimulation and it might be hard to hold full conversations. **A few examples:**

Situational

If she's at the bar: "What's your go-to drink? I want to try something new tonight."

Around the edge of the dancefloor/at the bar: "What do you think about the music here? Are you a big reggaeton/hip hop/pop fan?"

The "Dance Floor Hip Bump"

On the dancefloor: Give her a playful hip bump, smile, and take a step back. If she smiles back at you, gently take her hand, spin her, and start dancing. **To help you visualize this, check out an example of me doing the dance floor hip bump here:** https://bit.ly/hip-bump-flirting.

The "She's Leaving"

Use this one when it appears that she's about to leave the venue and it's your last shot:

"Hey, I just noticed you and I had to meet you quickly before you go." This can be great for grabbing quick phone numbers and shooting your shot before you miss your chance.

Weaving In Banter Early On

Banter is the playful, witty exchange that adds a spark to your interactions. It can help transition the conversation from boring small talk to something more fun and flirty, breaking through the initial awkwardness.

You want to start weaving this in after the initial conversation starter.

How to Weave in Banter

Let's look at some ways that you can weave banter into the early part of your interactions:

Guessing Her Origin or Background

You can start with a playful guess about where she might be from or what her background is. This is a great way to show interest without directly asking, and regardless of whether you get it right, it makes things more fun.

Some examples:

- "You have a vibe that's hard to pin down, but I'm getting strong West Coast energy. Or maybe I'm just hoping you'll say that you're from somewhere with great surf."

- "You don't strike me as someone who's spent their life just in one place. You've got a big 'city girl' kind of vibe."

- "I'm usually good with accents, but yours has me stumped. It's not quite local but not quite foreign either. I'm guessing you're not from around here, are you?"

Guessing Her Profession

Not only does this add a spark of intrigue to your conversation but it also provides insight into her world. It's a playful way to demonstrate interest in her that goes beyond surface-level small talk.

Some examples:

- "You have an artistic flair about you. I'm getting strong graphic designer vibes, or maybe an architect? Definitely something that lets you channel creativity."
    - **Why It Works:** It shows that you're paying attention to her style and mannerisms, attributing them to creative and intellectually stimulating professions.

- "There's a decisiveness in your eye. I'm torn between thinking you're a lawyer who's always three steps ahead or a CEO running her own startup."
    - **Why It Works:** This guess attributes qualities of leadership and intelligence to her, which can be flattering and thought provoking.

If you're in more of a nightlife setting, you can incorporate the surroundings to fuel your banter. **Examples:**

- "You like vodka? I can't believe it. I'm a tequila guy—this'll never work!"
    - **Why It Works:** It adds a playful little "push," which can be used in a push/pull dynamic.
- "Your drink choice says a lot about you. That looks like a 'taking over the world one sip at a time' kind of cocktail."
    - **Why It Works:** It's a fun way to comment on her drink choice while subtly complimenting her confidence or ambition.

Getting Her Contact Info

You've started the conversation and had some solid banter, and now you're in a good position to close things out and get her contact info.

Daytime interactions, like a chance meeting at the park or a quick chat in the coffee line, are typically brief. You're both on-the-go, so it's short and sweet (maybe one to five minutes). Recognizing the tempo of the interaction is key for properly getting her contact info.

The Setup

When the conversation reaches a natural high point and you're feeling that mutual vibe, it's time to pivot to the close. Start with something like, "Hey, I've got to meet a friend, but you seem like fun. Do you want to hang out sometime?"

If she says no, just say, "All good—take it as a compliment."

If she says yes, hand her your phone on the contact entry screen and say, "Cool. Add your number here and we'll make it happen."

Or, if you have an optimized Instagram (if you're not sure if it's optimized, then it's not—you can't "luck" your way into an attractive IG), you can opt for getting her IG instead. In this case, it's actually better if *you* put it into her phone.

Once she agrees, the way to do it is to say, "Cool. Here—search my IG"—you can type it yourself or have her type it. Ideally you're typing it, and you can just go in, follow yourself, and then drop yourself a quick direct message (like an emoji) from her account. That way, she'll immediately see your message when you DM her, and it won't go to the "Message Requests" tab.

You'll want to get her contact info in the first interaction every time, *except* for situations where you know that you're very likely to see her again.

For example, at the gym when you two typically go on the same days or times, or at a dance class where you see each other once a week or a few times a month.

In cases like those, it's okay to build rapport the first time and then go for the contact info on your second or third conversation when she shows signs of interest. This helps you uphold your reputation and be a little more calculated.

Closing Out Nightlife Interactions

Nightlife scenarios, in contrast, can be brief at the beginning of the night when you're first building momentum. You might have three or four quick interactions of a few minutes (or even less), where you end by exchanging contact info.

But as the night progresses, you'll typically find yourself in longer interactions. In these cases, it's key to weave in the flirting that's been throughout this book. You also want to lead and "make it real."

Making it real means making a genuine connection beyond just the fun flirting. And yes—there *is* time to do this in nightlife interactions. Generally, it's best to take her to a quieter part of the venue where you can talk a little deeper and get to know her without all the crazy loud music. This will solidify the interaction more and make it a more memorable experience for her, and it's key if you want to minimize the chances of her flaking or ghosting you the next day.

To make it real, you can ask questions like:

- "What brought you to this city?"
- "What do you like to do for fun?"
- "What was your last big adventure?"
- "If you could wake up anywhere in the world tomorrow, where would it be?"

When she poses the questions back to you, you can relate with quick stories about your own life before turning the conversation back over to her.

And when it comes to leading, I'm referring to guiding the interaction from beginning to end toward your desired outcome. You can do things like move her throughout different parts of the venue, like the dancefloor, the bar, and quieter areas. The more she follows your lead, the more invested she becomes in the interaction, allowing you to make bigger asks.

To properly lead well, do the following:

- Know where you're going. Have a desired outcome in mind.

- Know your logistics—where you're staying, when you need to wake up, and how you'll get home.
- Build compliance. Basically, this refers to when a girl does what you want her to be doing.
    - **For example**, if you stop her to talk and she stops and listens, or if you lead her somewhere and she follows. You can give her "compliance tests" like these throughout the interaction to get an idea of where you stand.

Let's look at a few examples of leading in action:

- Grabbing a drink with her: "You're fun. Let's go grab a drink at the bar."
- Taking her to the lounge area for easier conversation: "Let's go hang out in the lounge—it's super chill over there."
- Going out for fresh air: "Let's get outside for a second—it's kinda stuffy in here."
- The dance floor to get a little more physical: "This song is awesome—let's hit the dance floor."
- You can also simply hold her hand as you lead her through a crowd.

Keep in mind that by going for the smaller asks (like "Let's go to the dance floor"), you give yourself a better chance to get a "yes" for the bigger asks (such as "Let's go back to my place").

If she shuts down your first few compliance tests, consider moving on. In those cases, it saves you time and allows you to meet other girls who you *will* click with.

As far as closing in nightlife scenarios goes, if you're going for the contact info, you can use the same kind of ask as the daytime close. It just might be a longer interaction and therefore more solidified (if you've done things right).

If you're looking to keep the night going at your place or hers and you leave the venue together, the following are some easy phrases to use (but make sure that you've built a good amount of compliance before trying them):

The Simple "Crazy, Stupid, Love" Close

You: "Do you want to get out of here?

Her: "Sure."

This seems simple, but if she likes you, if she's invested in the interaction, and if you've led well, she'll be more open to it than you think.

The "Adventure" Close

You: "Let's get out of here."

Her: "Okay, what do you want to do?"

You: "You up for an adventure?"

Her: "Yes."

You: "Cool—follow me."

Then go outside together, let her know that you live nearby, and call an Uber or a taxi.

The "Let's Get Food" Close

Maybe the night's coming to an end, but you can tell that she's not quite ready to go somewhere more private yet. That's when it helps to have a "bridge" location that allows you to switch venues and build more rapport. The simple way to do this is go for food after the bar—something quick like a slice or two of pizza is perfect. From there, you can invite her to somewhere private. You can initiate this with something like:

You: "There's a great pizza joint down the street. You want to grab a slice?"

Her: "Sure!"

Key Takeaways

- **Leverage Your Environment:** Use situational openers to start conversations—they feel smoother and demonstrate your ability to be observant and quick-witted.

- **Adapt to the Context:** The approach you use can vary based on where you are. For everyday settings like streets or parks, direct openers can be more effective, as they show confidence and clarity. In social environments like bars or clubs, situational openers can help you break the ice.

- **Banter is Key:** Early on in the interaction, weave in playful banter. An example of this could be guessing her background or profession in a light-hearted way.

- **Close with Confidence:** Unless you know that you're likely to see her again (like in a gym setting), go for the contact info in the first interaction. Ask if she wants to hang out sometime, and then get her number or exchange Instagram accounts (but only if your IG is optimized).

- **Know When and How to Lead:** Especially in longer nightlife interactions, it's key to lead the interaction purposefully. This includes moving her through different parts of the venue and building compliance with smaller requests before making larger ones, like suggesting heading back to your place or hers.

How to Flirt on Dates

Think about it: First-date flirting is actually the easiest kind. Why? She's already there with you. That means that she saw something in you—a spark, a hint of intrigue—something that made her think, "Yeah, this could be interesting. "

She's stepped into the ring with you, and that's half the battle won. This isn't a cold call; it's more like being handed a warm lead. At this point, it's not about proving your worth from square one—it's about building on the intrigue that's already there.

Let's examine how to make the most of it, have a solid first date, and infuse great flirting skills along the way.

The Goals of a First Date

First dates are basically a testing ground to see if you have chemistry with a girl. With this in mind, there are four goals:

1. Get Clarity on Compatibility

Sure, she caught your eye—but does she catch your vibe? Use this opportunity to see if there's more than just physical attraction. Does the conversation flow? Do your values align? Is there a spark when you share stories and ideas? Do you want the same things? Or does it all feel a little flat and forced?

And, most of all, is it worth a second date to continue getting to know each other?

2. Make It Cost-Effective

The point of becoming skilled at flirting isn't to go on five dates a week—it's to be able to easily have fun interactions, attract women, and be in control of your dating life. That said, you may actually *want* five dates every week, which is great, or you might be content with just a few dates a month, and that's fine too. The point is that you're able to achieve what you want.

With that in mind, if you're going on dates somewhat often, you need to make it sustainable. A $200 dinner date a few nights a week (or month) probably won't be worth it—nor is it necessary.

Instead, make your dates cost-effective. Opt for venues and date ideas that allow for solid conversation without the pressure of racking up an expensive bill. You can save that Michelin-starred restaurant for when she's actually your girlfriend.

3. Enjoy the Date & Have Fun!

If you're not enjoying yourself, what's the point? The goal is to enjoy each other's company. After all, this isn't a job interview—it's a chance to connect and have a good time.

Find joy in the little things during the date: a funny observation, a shared interest, or a quirky anecdote—all the things that are involved with getting to know somebody new. This can create a memorable experience for both of you.

Plus, you get a chance to try some of the new flirting techniques you learned here in this book, and that's a win!

4. Set the Stage for More

Whether it's another date or something more casual, leave the door open for future interactions. First dates aren't always about finding "The One"—sometimes they're just about exploring what could be. Yes, there's the possibility that she could be your next girlfriend. Or maybe she's cool but you don't click on a romantic level, and she could actually introduce you to her *friend* who becomes your next girlfriend! Or maybe it's more of a casual hookup situation. Keep your mind and your options open.

Cheap & Simple First Date Ideas

To accomplish those four goals above, you don't need to have some kind of amazing first date idea. In fact, there are only really two first date ideas you should have in your arsenal, except for some rare exceptions.

1. The Bar Date

Bars provide a perfect first date atmosphere—as long as you choose the right one.

You want a venue where you can hear each other but still feel the buzz of the nightlife. The right bar sets a mood that's casual yet intimate, a vibe that's perfect for getting to know each other without the pressure.

And if you don't drink? No problem. I don't drink anymore either. You can go somewhere with mocktails so that you can avoid the alcohol but still enjoy the benefits of the vibe.

Bonus points if the bar has a billiards table or darts—these give you an extra activity and are an easy way to lead her around the venue and get to know her more.

The ideal time for bar dates is weeknights starting from around 7 or 8 pm. It's not as packed as on a weekend but there should still be a decent crowd, setting the tone for a chill evening.

Choose a bar on the cheaper side (or one with daily drink discounts) if you're going on lots of dates so that you can keep costs low.

2. The Coffee & a Walk Date

This is an easy, chill, and inexpensive date idea if you want to mix in some daytime dates.

An ideal coffee shop has an easy-going vibe, and it's a perfect place to start. It's low investment, both in time and money, which makes saying yes easy for her, too. Plus, coffee offers a laid-back setting to get the date rolling.

Post-coffee, take the date outside. A walk through a bustling downtown area or a stroll by the lake gives you a cool backdrop for your date. It keeps things moving, both literally and conversationally.

Flirting on the First Date

Start off by greeting her outside the venue with a warm smile and a genuine but quick hug—this sets the tone for the rest of the date.

Then lead her into the venue, and once inside, sit next to her rather than across from her. This makes it easier to flirt and use physical touch, and it makes it feel less like an interview.

Once you're settled in, you can start rolling out some of the conversations and flirting strategies laid out earlier in this book.

Make It Flirty from the Start

You can ask something simple like, "How's your day been?" or "How was the drive here?" Her answers may give you opportunities to drop a few light, playful teases right away.

For example:

"How's your day been so far?" Her: (explains a busy day filled with a bunch of activities) You: "Wow—you've been crushing it today, huh? I might need to take notes."

Her: (explains a relaxed day) You: "Keeping it Zen, huh? We're going to have to add a little excitement into your days."

"How was your drive in?" Her: (talks about all the traffic) You: "You survived city traffic without losing your cool? I'm impressed!"

Her: (says it was a smooth drive) You: "Look at you, dodging traffic. I might need to take you with me on my drive to work."

Dive Deep & Sprinkle in Some Flirting

Once you get past some of the initial pleasantries and teasing, you can get to know her a bit.

Below are some example questions you can ask:

Exploring Her Background:

- "What was your favorite thing about growing up in (her hometown)?"
- "If you could bring one aspect of your hometown here, what would it be?"

- "What's one thing you miss about your hometown?"
- "What brought you here in the first place?"
- (if you both grew up in the same city) "What made you want to stick around?"

Understanding Her Career Choices:

- "Was working in (her field) always your plan, or did you stumble into it by chance?"
- "What got you interested in your field?"
- "What do you enjoy most about what you do?"
- "If you weren't doing this, what would be your dream job?"

Getting to Know Her Hobbies and Passions

- "What kinds of things are you most passionate about?"
- "What makes you so passionate about (her passion)?"
- "How do you feel when you're following that passion?"
- "What do you like to do for fun?"
- "What do you love about (what she loves to do)?"

Travel & Adventure

- "If you could wake up anywhere in the world tomorrow, where would it be?"

- "What's your favorite travel story?"
- "What's your favorite travel destination you've visited?"
- "What's the last big adventure you've gone on?"

Other Fun Questions

- "What kind of music do you love to dance to?"
- "What's something that I wouldn't guess about you?"
- "What's your favorite food?"
- "What's your favorite meal to cook?"
- "What's your favorite dessert?"

Recap of Flirty Questions to Use

- "What do you find sexy in a guy?"
- "What kinds of things make you laugh the hardest?"
- "What's the worst first date you've ever been on?"

Obviously, you don't want to ask these questions all in a row—instead, use a few of them throughout the conversation to get to know her. With each question, actively listen and relate back with your own experiences and thoughts. Then follow up and get to the next layer.

For example, if she tells you what she wanted to be when she grew up (but ended up going in a different direction), you can ask what made her decide to move away from that—and there may even be some room to give her a little motivation to try it again. What's more, many of these questions will give you fodder to tease and flirt with her.

For example:

Hometown Teasing

You: "What was your favorite thing about growing up in (her hometown)?" Her: (mentions loving the local music scene) You: "You were totally the rebel girl sneaking out to concerts as a teenager, weren't you?"

Food Future Projection

You: "What's your favorite meal to cook?" Her: (talks about her favorite dish to cook) You: "Sounds delicious. All right—we'll have to have a cooking night then. You cook, I'll bring the wine, and we'll call it a perfect night in. Fair warning, though: I'm a tough critic in the kitchen."

The Salsa Innuendo

You: "What kind of music do you love to dance to?" Her: (talks about loving salsa dancing) You: "Ah, so you've got some rhythm—that's important for a lot of things. I like that. I've got a few salsa dancing moves under my belt, too. We'll have to hit the dance floor one day!"

Keep in mind that on first dates, you'll be diving deep, weaving in flirting, and gently guiding things forward. Everything she tells you is a potential new conversation thread that you can use to flirt or get to know her on a deeper level. Remember to use some of the flirting techniques uncovered in this book as well.

Use Physical Flirting Throughout

So far, we've examined the importance of physical touch and flirting, but let's take a quick look into how to do it specifically on first dates.

First, why is physical touch important on the first date? It accomplishes a number of things:

- **Breaks the Touch Barrier:** Early on, casual touches (like greeting her with a hug or playfully touching her arm during a joke) can break the initial barrier, making more intimate touches (like putting your hand on her leg or going for a quick kiss) feel more natural later.

- **Creates Comfort and Connection:** Physical touch creates a sense of closeness and shared intimacy.

- **Tests her investment:** Does she freeze up with your touch, act neutral, or melt into it? Her reaction tells you a lot about her current interest and investment levels, and it also lets you know how ready she is to escalate things further.

- **Shows Dominance:** A guy who isn't afraid to get physical and go for what he wants is much more attractive than the guy who overthinks every single move.

Below are some ways that you can add physical touch into your dates:

- **The Greeting:** Start with the quick, warm hug described earlier.

- **Light, Casual Touches:** Look for natural opportunities for touch at high points, like when you're both laughing.

    - **For example**, you can gently nudge her arm when teasing her or give her a high five (and see if she clasps your fingers).

- **Guiding Gestures:** If you're moving to a new location or working your way through a crowd, guide her with a light touch on the small of her back.

- **Shared Activities:** You can do things that naturally require touch, like jokingly testing her biceps strength, comparing hand sizes (just make sure that you have bigger hands than her), or gently grasping her hand and asking about her rings or other jewelry.

- **Subtle Escalation:** If she's responding positively to light contact, you might touch her hair while complimenting it or briefly place your hand on her knee during a deeper part of the conversation. Always be mindful of her reactions, and back off if she seems stiff or freezes up.

- **The Quick Kiss:** Give her the quick three-to-five-second kiss mentioned earlier, and be the first one to pull back.

Key Takeaways

- **Recognize Her Interest:** Her presence on the date is already a sign of interest. She's intrigued and so the stage is set for you—not to prove your worth but to build on the existing attraction.

- **Cost-Effective Dates Matter:** Keep dates affordable—think coffee and a walk or drinks at a bar. There's no need to overdo it by insisting on an expensive dinner.

- **Flirting Helps Enhance the Connection:** Use teasing, playful banter, as well as deeper conversation topics to create a more in-depth exchange. Mix genuine curiosity with light-hearted teasing to keep the mood fun.

- **Leading the Interaction:** Guide the date from the start—from the greeting hug to choosing where to sit. This sets the tone and makes you come across confidently.

- **Be Aware of Her Responses:** Pay attention to her reactions to both your conversation and physical advances. Her comfort levels will let you know the right time to escalate things.

Flirting With a Group

The idea of flirting with or even approaching a group of girls may seem daunting, especially if you get anxious about talking to a single girl. But with the right approach and mindset, it's easier than you might think.

Let's get into how to meet women in groups and weave flirting in along the way.

Reframing the Group Approach

Let's get something straight: Walking up to a group of girls might feel like you're stepping into the lion's den, but here's a hot take—not only is it completely doable but it's often easier than talking to a girl solo, and it can even be more fun. Here's why:

It Provides a Conversational Buffer

Think about it. In a one-on-one situation, the spotlight's all on you to keep the conversation flowing. But in a group? You've got multiple women bouncing off each other, making the interaction more dynamic and less about you having to carry the whole show. It's like having a safety net—the girls can talk among themselves, which gives you room to observe, chip in, and steer the conversation forward.

Showcase Your Social Savvy

Sure, it can be a bit of a hurdle to get the whole group to warm up to you, but once they do, you're golden. Winning over the group often means that you've passed a collective test of coolness—it's like getting multiple stamps of approval from her friends, which makes narrowing in on the girl you're into a smoother ride.

You've Got a Head Start

Walking up to a group of girls by yourself might seem like a mission for two, but here's where the solo approach has its perks. It shows confidence and self-assuredness. Strolling in there without backup sends a message that you're confident in your own skin, and that's a major turn on. Plus, once you hold things down for a few minutes and win the group over, it's easy for your friends to join in and play good wingmen.

Understanding Group Dynamics

There are a few different group dynamics you'll come into contact with, and you'll want to navigate each of them a little differently. Let's take a look at the main ones:

The Duo

This is actually slightly more challenging than a group of three or more girls. It can feel like you're interrupting a private party, making it harder to isolate the girl you like. After all, it's not the most savvy move to take her away and leave her friend all alone.

The move here is to give them *both* the spotlight. If you're in a nightlife setting, you can approach with something simple, like, "You girls look like fun. How's your night going?" Make sure that you bring a smile and positive energy when you do this.

If it's during the day, the easiest thing is to either go with something situational or ask for directions, getting them both involved in the conversation.

For example: "Hey, I know this is a little random, but y'all seem hip and like you know the area. I'm looking for a good coffee place here—do you have any recommendations?"

Keep in mind that in two-girl groups, you've basically got to do everything together. If you're getting a drink, checking out a different area of the venue, or going on a mini adventure, you've got to bring the friend along—at least until she gets picked off by another opportunistic guy. And if she's attractive, this often does happen.

The Larger Group

With three or more girls, the dynamic shifts. Isolating your girl becomes a greater possibility, as her friends will still have company with each other. In nightlife venues, you can use the same "You guys look like fun" line, as it works well.

If it's during the day, you can ask for directions and then interlude by saying that they seem like fun, and then keep the conversation going. Or, if you're feeling courageous, you can simply go direct and say, "Excuse me, ladies—I know this is random, but I saw your friend walking here and I thought that she was the most beautiful girl I've seen all day, and so I had to meet her quickly." Then turn to the friend, introduce yourself, and turn back to the group and ask, "What are you ladies up to?" This might seem a little far-fetched, but if done smoothly, it can work like a charm.

Check out a clip of me doing this with a group of girls on the Venice Beach boardwalk here: https://bit.ly/group-approaching.

The Mixed Group

If you're beginner level, so to speak, I'd recommend sticking with girl-only groups until you get some experience under your belt. Once you do, you'll start recognizing more opportunities and become more comfortable stepping into them.

Also, you just might see a beautiful girl you want to talk to but she's flanked by a guy or two in her group. Most guys would shy away from this, but now you'll have the skills and awareness to handle it.

The best way to approach the mixed group is by starting with the guys. You can start by dropping a compliment—something as simple as saying you like their shirt, shoes, or style, and giving them a "cheers." Once you chop it up with the guys for a couple of minutes, you can ask how they know the rest of the group. This gives you an understanding of the group dynamic, as well as which girls are off limits (if any).

Once they introduce you to the rest of the group, you can cautiously work your way in. Just don't completely ignore the guys. Keep them involved in the conversation, at least for the early stages, and this will help you earn their trust.

Keep in mind that not all mixed groups will be open to mingling with you. Some guys will see what you're doing immediately and completely shut you down. The better your vibe, the more open groups will generally be to meeting you.

Flirting During Group Interactions

Here's a key thing to remember in group interactions: If the friends don't like or trust you, it'll be hard to make anything happen—even if your girl is into you.

You need to keep the group involved and engaged early on so as to not make it seem like you're only interested in their friend and don't care about them at all.

How to Flirt Like a Pro in Group Settings

Flirting with a group is a bit like you're the conductor of an orchestra—you've got to harmonize different elements and personalities to create a symphony. And it all starts from the very beginning.

Engage The Whole Group Initially

- **Strategy:** Start by engaging the entire group to avoid coming off as rude or too direct. This establishes you as friendly and socially savvy. You'd likely be surprised how many guys single out the girl they like from the start and ignore everyone else. Bad move.

- **Example:** Walk up to the group and, with a playful tone, say, "Alright, I need a quick opinion here. Who's the best at giving advice on (a light topic like music, movies, etc.)?"

Playfully Involve the Group in Flirting

- **Strategy:** Use the group's dynamics to your advantage. Make light-hearted assumptions or playful guesses that include everyone.

- **Example:** Pointing to the girl you're interested in, turn to her friends and playfully say, "She's a Scorpio, isn't she?" or "She's the troublemaker of the group, isn't she?"

Discover the Relationship Dynamics

- **Strategy:** Find out how the group knows each other, which gives you valuable info (are they best friends, family, coworkers?). They may act differently according to the group dynamic and,
    - **For example**, be more reserved around other coworkers (but not always!). Plus, you can tease them about the relationship dynamic.
- **Example 1:**
    - You: "So how do you guys all know each other?"
    - Them: (explains that they're co-workers)
    - You: "Okay, so who's the one who's always stealing all the lunches from the fridge?"
- **Example 2:**
    - If it seems like they're newer acquaintances, you can tease them with something fun like, "You all have this 'we just met but we're already friends' energy. Tinder group date?"

Along with these examples, you also have the "best friend test," in which you simply ask, "You guys are best friends, aren't you?" They'll usually say, "Yes! How'd you know?!" and you can run with it from there.

While doing all of this, you can essentially treat the group as one big flirting interaction. Make eye contact with all of them, lightly flirt, and ask some light connecting questions. Then you can bring it back to the girl you like when it's possible. This helps you win over the group and get their approval, and it also gives you the best chance to win over the one you like.

Getting Alone Time with Your Girl

I'll be real with you: It's pretty fun once you really get a handle on managing group flirting dynamics. It kind of makes you feel unstoppable and gives you the confidence of knowing that no group or interaction is off limits.

But you're not here because it's fun to handle group dynamics—you're here because you want to get the girl! And to do that, you've got to find a way to isolate her away from the group and get some alone time.

Transitioning from the Group to One on One

- **Strategy:** After about five to ten minutes of group engagement, it's time to focus on your girl. The key here is to do it in a way that feels natural and unforced.

- **Approach:** Casually suggest an activity that naturally requires fewer people. For instance, say to her, "Hey, have you tried the spicy margarita at the bar here? Let's go grab one—I've heard good things about it." This approach is non-threatening and offers a good reason to separate from the group, even just momentarily. You can even ask permission from the group if you want to, and playfully say something like, "You guys cool if I steal your friend to grab a drink for a few minutes? I promise I'll bring her back safe." If you've managed the group dynamics as suggested above, they should be totally cool with it.

Handling a Duo: When It's Her & Her Friend

- **Strategy:** In case you're dealing with two girls, you don't want to leave one of them hanging—that's a fast track to making a bad impression.

- **Approach:** Engage both of them in the transition. For instance, "You guys must try the mojitos here. Let's go—I'll show you." This keeps the vibe friendly and inclusive, and it also shows that you're considerate of her friend. Hopefully at some point, another guy approaches the friend. If not, you can entertain them both, and if they're feeling adventurous, you may have an opportunity to go somewhere in private with them both (although this is a little more of an advanced strategy). If you're not at that level yet, you can always work out the logistics, make sure that the friend can get home safe at the end of the night, and then you'll have some alone time with your girl.

The Back-and-Forth Dance: Building Investment

- **Tactic:** Once you've isolated her, it's not necessarily about staying away from the group for the rest of the night. Instead, you can use the opportunity to deepen your connection and then rejoin the group. This shows that you're social and respectful of her time with friends.

- **Execution:** After a bit of one-on-one time, suggest rejoining her friends. "Let's head back to your group—I don't want them thinking that I've kidnapped you." This balance between private and group interaction helps you build trust and exhibit your social savviness. You can have a bit of back-and-forth like this throughout the night, isolating and then rejoining the group.

Sealing the Deal

- **Final Move:** As the night progresses and you feel a strong connection, you can consider taking things to the next level.

- **Suggestion:** If things are going well and she's following your lead, you might say, "I know this great spot nearby with an incredible view. Let's get out of here and check it out." It's important to read her cues—her level of comfort with you tells you everything you need to know.

Final Pointers for Groups

- **Respect the Friends:** Always acknowledge and respect her friends. Winning them over is just as important as winning your girl. If her friend goes full "Karen" on you because of your sloppy approach, you're in for a rough time.

- **Maintain a Connection with the Group:** Keep touching base with the group throughout the night. It shows that you're considerate and not just there for a quick pick up.

- **Identify the "Leader" of the Group:** The "alpha" of the group will have the biggest influence over the others. If you get *her* on your side, everything else becomes easier.

- **Plan Your Exit (If needed):** If the vibe isn't right or if the group isn't receptive to your presence, be ready to gracefully exit the conversation. A simple "Great chatting with you—enjoy your evening!" is all you need.

- **Smooth Transitions:** Watch for opportunities in the conversation where you can naturally shift your focus to the girl you like.

    - **For example,** if she mentions something that you're also interested in, use that as a segue.

Key Takeaways

- **Embrace the Group Dynamic:** Think approaching a group is scary? Flip the script and make it an opportunity. Chatting with a group takes the pressure off of you to keep the conversation going all by yourself.

- **Understand Different Group Setups:** Each group dynamic needs its own playbook. Duos are a balancing act, so you need to include both of them to avoid leaving anyone out. Larger groups? You've got more wiggle room to focus on and isolate the girl you're interested in, but make sure that you're engaging the whole group first. Mixed company? Make friends with the guys to build trust.

- **Flirting Tactics for Groups:** Use playful banter or make light-hearted guesses about the group or your girl. This will make everyone's night more fun, and the group will be glad they met you.

- **Smooth Moves for One-on-One Time:** Got the group's approval? Time for some alone time with your girl. Suggest a side adventure—maybe a drink or a dance. Keep it laid back and casual, like it's just another fun twist in the night.

- **Sealing the Deal:** As the night goes on, suggest a change of scenery if you and your girl are vibing. It could be a quiet corner in the venue or a different spot altogether. The key? Just make sure that she's invested and following your lead before going in for the ask.

Flirting Over Text & Dating Apps

Earlier in this book, we examined how women flirt over text messages, which showed you how to identify if a girl is interested and receptive.

But many guys struggle when it comes to texting. And after working with thousands of clients through dating coaching, I've seen *a lot* of guys make easily preventable texting errors that end up costing them dates.

This chapter will give you a great foundation with which to text women the right way so that you can stop missing out on opportunities.

The 5 Texting Principles

1. Use Her Name

It's simple psychology—hearing (or reading) her name triggers a unique reaction in her brain, creating a sense of familiarity and comfort. This instantly personalizes your conversation and makes her feel like she's not just another contact in your phone. Kick off a new text thread by using her name, something along the lines of, "Hey Emily, it's (your name). I'm still looking for that perfect avocado."

2. Sound Smart but Casual

Well-written texts signal that you're intelligent and mature, while sloppy texts signal the opposite and can sometimes be a dealbreaker. You definitely want to avoid grammar mistakes and awkward formatting. That said, being too formal can be a buzzkill. You're not penning a college essay here.

The happy medium is smart but casual, like you're chatting with a friend you respect. No spelling mistakes, correct grammar and formatting, but not overly formal.

For example:

Too formal: "Hello (her name), let's go for a drink date this week. Are you going to be available on Tuesday or Thursday?"

Just right: "Hey (her name), let's grab drinks this week. You free Tuesday or Thursday?"

3. Match Her Response Time (To a Point)

If she takes hours to respond, and then once she does you text back within two minutes, you're going to seem a bit needy. Instead, match the tempo—if she takes 30 minutes to respond, then you should take anywhere from 20 to 40 minutes. This subtly communicates that you've got a life beyond your phone screen. But this doesn't mean that you should play games; if she's responsive and quick, feel free to keep the pace. Just avoid instant replies every time, as it can come off as you being too available.

But if she takes a day or two to respond, you won't be able to mirror that—it'll make for a pretty long and drawn-out conversation. Instead, in this case, respond a bit faster (maybe 30 minutes later) and keep it strictly logistical. Try to set up that date! Forget about small talk and building rapport at this point.

4. Less is More

You're not Will Shakespeare trying to write a love letter here—you don't need to engage in long, in-depth text conversations. The longer your texts, the harder it is to transition into an in-person meet up, and the more likely you are to be the "pen pal" stuck in the friendzone.

You should aim to go for the meet-up or date after you each send anywhere between four to seven texts. Any longer than that and you risk killing the tension and losing the girl. Also, avoid double and triple texting. If she doesn't respond for a bit, let it sit and give her a chance. Panicking and sending multiple texts will generally make you come off as needy.

5. Every Text Has a Purpose

Each you send should be, in some way, moving you closer to the next hangout. You don't need to get "too cute" and weave in all these intricate bits of flirting or ask her the perfect question. None of that is going to help and, in a lot of cases, can lead to over-validating the girl to the point where she's not that excited to hang with you anymore.

Instead, aim to push the conversation toward a meet-up. Cut out the filler questions and focus on building up to that date. Before sending a message, ask yourself, "Is this text moving me closer to my goal?" If it's not clearly serving a purpose, don't send it.

For example, before the first date, you wouldn't want to text her, "Anyway, what places have you always wanted to travel to?" That's a question you'd ask on the first date. But if she texts *you* a question like that, you could say, "More fun to talk about that over drinks (wink emoji). How's tomorrow or Thursday sound?"

Flirting Over Text Before the First Date

At this point, you don't have much buy-in or investment from the girl yet, especially if you've only had a quick interaction with her. That said, the stronger your communication and flirting fundamentals are, the more excited she'll be to meet you. You'll have a little wiggle room to make some mistakes. But either way, it's better to have a clean, easy texting plan you can use for light banter, followed by asking her out.

Once you get her number and while you're still with her, text her your name and location. If you're meeting her at the grocery store, you'd just text, "Mark - supermarket" and make sure that it went through on her phone. Then tell her it was good to meet her and that you'll text her later on. This sets expectations and keeps things simple.

If you're in a nightlife setting and you exchange Instagrams, you can take a quick smiling selfie of the two of you and have that be the first direct message. And if you're feeling confident, you can tell her to kiss you on the cheek in the picture.

And from there, let it sit for a bit—you'll want to wait before sending her the second text. If you met her during the day (say, before 5 pm), you can text her later that evening after 8 pm. If you met her at night (any time after 5 pm), you can text her the next day around noon.

That second text will be the "callback humor" text. This jogs her memory of who you are and brings back the positive emotions she felt when she met you. This is a lot better than the "Hey, how are you?" or "Did you have fun last night?" texts that most guys send. It'll help you stand out—*and* get a response.

Callback Humor in Action

Below are some examples to build off of. Keep in mind that you can use a subtle laughing emoji at the end of the texts to spice them up a bit. But remember not to overdo it—don't use emojis in every text or multiple emojis at a time.

Premise: You talked to her about how much the two of you like Mexican food.

Callback Text: "Hey (her name), fun meeting you last night. I've been craving breakfast tacos ever since we talked."

Premise: You asked for directions to Starbucks, then told her that you thought she was cute.

Callback Text: "Hey (her name), honestly never found Starbucks yesterday. Still searching for my coffee."

Premise: You joked about travel destinations.

Callback Text: "Hey (her name), caught myself planning our imaginary trip to Rome over breakfast. Hope you're ready for some gelato and history! "

Premise: You met at the gym and she gave you some leg workout tips.

Callback Text: "Hey (her name), my legs are still killing me from that workout. Thanks for that! "

Bridging the Conversation

Once you've dropped some callback humor and she's responded well, you've got to keep the conversation moving forward. This is your "bridge."

To bridge the conversation, simply add value and then ask about her day.

For example:

Callback Text: "Hey (her name), caught myself planning our imaginary trip to Rome over breakfast. Hope you're ready for some gelato and history! "

Her Response: "Haha, I'm already fantasizing about pasta!"

Your Bridge: "Get that appetite going, ha. Anyway, I just got a great workout in (this adds value). How's your Thursday going?"

You basically insert some quick, interesting info about your day (the value) and then ask about hers. This gives her something to work with. **Some other value phrases could be:**

- "Currently blasting (famous music artist) on the way to the gym."
- "Just hit the beach and got an early surf in."
- "Just crushed my last bit of work for the day."
- "Currently walking through downtown and taking in some sun."

Once she responds to that, there may be one more line of banter you can use, but it actually may not be needed depending on her response.

If she seems interested, you can go right for the date from there:

"Anyway, you seem like fun. Let's grab a drink this week. You free Tuesday or Thursday?"

Keep the following in mind: When you suggest a date, never call it a "date," as it can feel a bit too formal. Also, always give her two options for when to meet, and if neither of those work for her, she can suggest another day. When picking these days, aim to set the date up within two to four days, as the "flake rate" can skyrocket if it's any longer than that.

Then, once you set up the date, make sure to confirm it the day before. This can just be a simple text like, "Hey (her name), we still all good for tomorrow at 7 pm at McCarthy's Pub?"

Once she confirms, you can then respond the day of and say, "Sounds good, see you there." This adds a little extra confirmation without needing to ask.

Confirming makes the date real in her mind, and so she'll be less likely to flake.

Flirting Over Text After the First Date

Once you've had a solid first date, you'll have more buy-in from here. But bear in mind that you can still screw things up with the wrong texts!

Here are a few mistakes you'll want to avoid:

- **Immediately Trying to Schedule the Next Date:** Going in for the second date right away makes you come off as way too eager and desperate. It's much better to give it a few days to breathe before asking again. You can still text with some callback humor the next day, but then let it sit before re-initiating the conversation and going for the hangout. So, if you sent callback humor on Tuesday and got a good response, wait until Thursday or Friday to reach out again (with the same format you used before the first date—bridge, banter, then ask) to plan the next one.

- **Becoming Her Texting Buddy:** Guys will have a great meet-up with a girl and then try to text her all the time afterwards. You guys *aren't* on that level yet. Doing this will just over validate her and get her less excited about the second date. Remember Dex's principle: "Be gone," as it definitely applies here.

- **Don't Panic:** If you don't get a response right away, stay calm and go on with your day. At this point, you've done your job, and the rest is on her.

A great way to reach out again if you haven't texted her in a few days is to send a quick ten-second video message. The key here is to record it with upbeat energy and tonality—it's a really solid way to stand out.

Check out this example of me recording a video message, and just follow the format: https://bit.ly/dave-video-text.

Flirting Over Text Three or More Dates In

At this point you've got a lot of buy in from her (as long as you've been running the dates well and using the flirting techniques we've covered).

You really don't need to do anything special here. You can follow the same format: callback humor after the date, some banter in between, and then planning the next hang out. There may be a little more banter in between as you hang out with her more and build rapport and comfort. The hangouts may start to happen gradually more frequently as well—and all of that is fine.

Ideally, after three to five dates and you've gotten intimate, she should be texting you a little more eagerly and coming up with date ideas herself. This isn't always the case, though—some girls text more than others, so don't sweat it either way.

How to Flirt in Online Dating

Flirting online is very similar to flirting over text, and many of the girls you text may be from online dating interactions anyway, so there's a lot of overlap.

The main difference is that you've got to get her engaged at the start before she's met you.

If you have a solid dating profile with optimized photos, this becomes far, far easier. It's even easier if you link your dating profile to your (optimized) Instagram account.

Your photos and profile will do much of the work for you. Great flirting won't make up for terrible photos, and great photos will give you more wiggle room to screw things up on the flirting. That's why, before anything else with online dating, you need to make sure that your photos, bio, and prompts are on point, or else this is all for naught.

If you want to understand what high-quality dating photos look like, check out the IG for Beast Photos: www.instagram.com/beastphotos_official. You can use this for posing, background, and style inspiration as well.

Aside from that, you might be wondering, "Once I match with a girl, then what do I do?" I could give you some go-to openers as examples, but that wouldn't make sense here. Every guy would just copy and paste them in and they'd become overused. And I don't want you getting called out for using some line that the last ten guys she's talked to have used! Instead, I'm going to give you the principles behind great initial messages so that it'll be easy for you to craft them in your own style.

The Anatomy of a Winning First Message

- **Easy to Respond To:** Don't try to be "too clever." This makes it harder for the girl to respond, because she'll feel as if she needs to come up with something clever, too. The easier your message is to respond to, the more likely it'll get a response, and that's the whole point—to get the conversation going.

- **Creates a Fun and Flirty Vibe:** You want to avoid the "friend zone" from the start, so your first message should create a flirty dynamic that'll help you get her attracted.

- **Stands Out (At Least a Little):** If you send the same types of messages that every other guy sends, you'll get the same types of responses (usually nothing). You don't need to do anything crazy—but just don't be so predictable. Always avoid "Hey, how are you?" messages.

One of the easiest things you can do is point out something from her profile or bio, and then use that as the initial message. This ensures that it's unique.

Once you've sent a solid first message and get a response, you can have a few lines of banter, similar to what we covered in the texting section above. Then, after four or five messages, ask if she wants to hang out. Once she says yes, grab her number or Instagram and move things off the app.

Key Takeaways

- **Follow the Texting Principles:** Use her name, sound smart but casual, match her response time, and text with a purpose.

- **Open with Callback Humor:** This helps jog her memory and brings up the positive emotions she associated with your initial conversation.

- **Use Texting Bridges:** After your callback humor text, shift to simple rapport-building questions, like asking about her day. This keeps the conversation moving forward and sets you up for suggesting a meet-up.

- **Confirm the Date the Day Before:** This helps you avoid getting stood up and flaked on, and it also shows respect for your time.

- **Texting After the Date:** The next day, send callback humor established during the date, but don't go for the second date right away. Let it sit for a few days, then re-initiate. Once she responds, you can start planning out the next date.

- **Online Dating Flirting:** Your first message should be fun, flirty, and somewhat unique. The easiest way to do this is to use something on her profile to start the conversation. Then, push for the date within the first four to six messages.

Part 4: How to Be a Natural at Flirting

The 10 Raw Skills That Make You Better at Flirting

There may have been moments throughout this book when you've thought, "That's awesome advice...but I'm not good at that!" or "That doesn't come naturally to me!"

But here's the thing: The beautiful part of flirting is that it's a skill. And like any skill, it can be learned, and there are certain things that you can do to accelerate that learning process.

This is where the raw skills of flirting come into play. The more you improve on each of these skills, the better you'll be at flirting and communication. And thankfully, these skills are all actually *fun* to learn.

I'll start by laying out the skills and explaining them. Then, in the next chapter, we'll examine how exactly you can develop each of these skills and truly become a natural at flirting.

1. Wittiness

When it comes to flirting, wittiness means that you can think quickly and come up with clever responses that add a spark to the conversation. It's about finding the fun, clever angle and using it to your advantage.

Wittiness keeps conversations lively and interesting, and it also makes your interactions memorable and engaging. It could be that innuendo you come up with on the spot that adds a little spice, or maybe that quick comeback when she tries to test you.

If you've got wittiness, everything else with flirting becomes easier.

One helpful technique to be more witty is to agree and exaggerate when she tests you.

For example, if she says, "You're too young for me," you could agree and exaggerate with something like, "Of course I am. I'll have to slow down a little so that you can keep up."

2. Reduced Self-Monitoring

But you can be witty in a platonic way, too, so that's not enough. You still need a little bit of an edge that turns your flirting from friendly to something more. And if you constantly filter yourself, you won't have that.

That's where reduced self-monitoring comes in. This is the ability to express yourself freely and spontaneously without over analyzing or excessively censoring yourself. It's an essential skill that involves lowering the filter that checks and modifies your behavior and speech when you're talking to women.

High levels of self-monitoring can make your conversations seem rehearsed, scripted, or artificial, but good flirting thrives on spontaneity and authenticity.

And here's a trade secret for you: If I had to point to just one thing that made me great at flirting so quickly, it's this very skill.

I started by completely removing my filter, which I had some success with but wasn't exactly the right move—I'd sometimes cross the line a little too often and offend people. So I added it back in at a low level, and it honestly elevated my flirting to new heights.

Most guys have a very heavy filter. This causes them to be self-conscious and more calculating, and it doesn't allow the interaction to flow.

As you lower your filter, your conversations will flow more smoothly and you'll come off with just the right amount of "edge."

There are many guys out there who are concerned about "running out of things to say." What's ironic is that you may know exactly what to say in the moment but you convince yourself that it's a bad idea. Just start by saying that "thing" and see how it goes!

3. Sense of Humor

Having a sense of humor isn't just about making someone laugh—it's more about viewing the world through a playful lens and bringing a little flavor and joy into interactions.

It shows that you don't take yourself too seriously and that you're always up for a little fun.

The point here isn't to be the "class clown" or constantly add jokes to the conversations—that can make you seem a little too goofy. It's more about sprinkling in some well-timed humor at different points throughout the conversation.

4. Storytelling

The world is run by stories—after all, it's how we communicate. And the guys who are the best with women are *great* storytellers.

When you master the art of storytelling, you can captivate people and really bring them into your world. And this is especially powerful when communicating with women.

You're able to convey and make her feel emotions, showcase your communication skills, and engage her imagination.

Start by having a few go-to stories that you tell on dates and in your interactions. Really perfect those stories—tell them to yourself in the mirror, record them, and flesh them out so that it becomes second nature to tell them. The best stories showcase attractive qualities about yourself without outright bragging, all while keeping the woman engaged and interested.

5. Presence

This is about more than just being physically there—it's also about being mentally and emotionally tuned in.

When you're present, you can pick up on her social cues and guide the conversation in the right direction, and you're not overthinking or overanalyzing. You just let it flow.

An average guy might talk to a girl and think, "I wonder if she likes me" or "I don't want to say the wrong thing!", but a present guy isn't concerned with that. He enjoys the moment, the beauty of the woman, and the interaction.

This presence builds trust and helps create intimacy. She can tell that you're fully tuned in, and she can relax a bit more in your presence.

6. Empathy

Great flirting requires a certain level of comfort. She's got to feel okay being a little vulnerable with you, and that's where empathy comes into play.

Basically, empathy is the ability to understand and share her feelings, and it's a key element in coming across with more warmth.

This allows you to tune into her emotional cues more. Is she hesitant, enthusiastic, amused, or intrigued? You can pick up on these cues and direct the conversation in the right way.

7. Self-Amusement

This skill comes back to having a playful approach to life and not taking yourself too seriously. Self-amusement boils down to being able to find joy and humor in your interactions—not solely for the entertainment of the girl but also for your own genuine enjoyment.

You're not "performing" or trying to impress. You're your own source of fun, and she's invited to join in. The beauty of this is that it takes the pressure off. She can choose to join in on the fun, but if not, it's her loss.

8. Self-Acceptance

If you're overloaded with insecurities, you'll have a hard time flirting well. You'll overthink everything, which will slow you down and make you seem stiff. You'll also have a tendency to mask your true self, and that'll hinder any connection that you're trying to build.

That's why self-acceptance is key. When you're genuinely okay with who you are, you can express yourself authentically without fear. You can make that joke, talk about your hobbies, and share your real perspective. And none of it will be a facade.

Plus, you'll be more resilient to rejection. If she doesn't like your flirting style or a certain tease that you make, it won't make you doubt yourself or your worth. You *know* that you're enough—despite what any woman may think. Self-acceptance gives you freedom and allows you to communicate in a way that other guys can't.

9. Leading

Most guys go into their interactions with literally zero idea of how they'll move things forward:

"It seems like she likes me. What do I do now?" "She's giving me a test. What does it mean?" They have no guiding structure or plan for what's going to happen when things go well—or when they go poorly. They just sort of do things and hope for the best, and this is a losing strategy.

When you're flirting, you should be gently guiding and leading the interaction somewhere. This could be toward getting her to invest more in the interaction, spiking her emotions, or even leading toward a physical location, like another venue or somewhere more private.

When you're leading, you've got some sort of logistics or goal in the back of your mind. You're still in the moment while flirting, but you know where you want things to end up.

10. Spontaneity

This is all about being creative and responsive in the moment, and even a little impulsive at times. It adds an element of surprise and keeps the women you're talking to on their toes. It makes you unpredictable, helping you to break their patterns and really engage with you.

Spontaneity could show up as a spur-of-the-moment, adventurous idea that you bring up, or as a quick joke or innuendo that you make.

Here's an example. Back in my early twenties, I took a trip to San Diego, and I found myself on a date with a beautiful girl on my last night there. But logistically, there was nowhere we could go to get intimate—her place was unavailable and I was staying at a friend's house.

So with nothing to lose, **I made a spontaneous move:** "Look, I think you're cool and I'm super attracted to you. I'm enjoying my time with you, but you know I'm going to be leaving tomorrow. So is it okay if I make a proposition that might seem a little crazy?"

"What is it?!" she laughed.

"What if we drive to the beach, lay out a blanket, and (get intimate) under the stars?" I asked, grinning. I figured I might as well shoot my shot.

"Oh my God!" she said, taken aback for a moment. "I've never done anything like that before, and we just met…"

"Yeah, I know it's a little crazy. I'm cool either way. If you want to continue the adventure, I'm up for that. And if not, it's been amazing hanging out," I said.

She paused for a second and laughed. And then:

"Well…I *do* have a sleeping bag in my car we could lay out…and there's this quiet beach we could drive to where nobody would bother us…"

"So…you want to make this adventure happen then?" I asked.

"You know what? Yes, let's do it!" she smiled.

Needless to say, that turned into a *very* memorable night.

Now, that's not a move that I'd typically recommend, and I'm guessing that it likely has a fairly low success rate. But sometimes the moment calls for a little spontaneity, and if you're willing to step up and go for it, you can have some amazing adventures.

It also illustrates just how much great flirting can change things. Had the flirting not been dialed in, there's no way that she would've been open to it. But because she felt that we were both on the same team and like I wasn't going to judge her, she was willing to do something out of the ordinary.

Spontaneity in your actions and words can help you give her unique experiences while making you memorable.

Now that we're at the end of this chapter, you might be thinking, "These are a lot of skills. How am I going to master all of these?" Thankfully, it's a lot simpler than you think, because many of these skills have overlap. There are a few quick daily and weekly activities that you can do to hone them in and become a natural at flirting. And that's exactly what we'll dive into in the next chapter.

Key Takeaways

- **Raw Skills:** There are certain things that just make you better at flirting. Once you get these raw skills down, flirting and banter will come naturally.

- **Develop Your Wit:** Quick, clever responses add fun to your flirting and keep her guessing.

- **Reduce Your Self-Monitoring:** When you lower your internal filter, you can express yourself more freely and authentically, allowing you to take more risks in your conversations.

- **Build Your Sense of Humor:** This allows you to add more fun and playfulness to your interactions without coming across as goofy.

- **Storytelling:** Have a few stories under your belt that you can bring out in your conversations.

- **Presence and Empathy:** These qualities help you to better pick up on social and emotional cues, encourage her to feel safe around you, and make the interaction more memorable.

- **Self-Amusement and Acceptance:** These help you reduce your fear of rejection, enjoy interactions more, and not be negatively impacted if a conversation doesn't go your way.

- **Leading:** This skill allows you to guide things forward so that you're flirting with a purpose.

- **Spontaneity:** Being spontaneous with your words and actions adds excitement. It makes your interactions more compelling and opens the door to fun, shared adventures with women.

How to Build the Raw Flirting Skills and Become a Natural with Women

Now that you know the key raw flirting skills, you're likely wondering how to actually build them.

As I promised in the last chapter, the skills are actually pretty fun and easy to learn. And they won't just help you with flirting—they'll also help you become a better communicator, more confident, and more decisive.

To be fair, you may look at some of these suggestions and wonder, "What the heck is this guy talking about?" or "That seems weird!"

But hey—all I ask is for you to keep an open mind. I've done all of these activities myself, taught them to thousands of men, and seen them make a huge impact firsthand.

Stand-Up Comedy & Improv

My father, John Perrotta, happens to be a stand-up comic. He's opened for some of the biggest comics in the game, from Bill Burr to Dane Cook and many more. If you've been to any comedy shows in the New England area, you may have heard of him. He's known as the "Italian Don Rickles."

Don Rickles is a legendary comedian widely known for his sharp wit and crowd work. And just like Don, my father *loves* to work the crowd. He'll go up and down the room and ask people what they do for work, how they know each other, and deliver quick quips along the way—all while bringing plenty of energy and basically having the presence of a mob boss. Ironically, he's also known as "The Godfather" of Rhode Island comedy.

The point of all this isn't to promote my dad (though you might want to see one of his shows if you find yourself in New England!). It's to say that ever since I can remember, I was attending my dad's stand-up comedy shows and watching him do crowd work, as well as bearing witness to all the other comics he brought up along the way.

And it had a *big* impact on the way I communicate myself, even if I didn't realize it at the time. I'd pick up on the way he teased the crowd and would come to tease women in a similar way as I got older. I adopted his quick wit and wordplay as well, and I learned to weave them into fun innuendos and use wit to pass any woman's tests.

Looking back, this was a big part of the reason that I was able to "get good" with women faster than most. It was because I'd already built a lot of the raw skills of flirting by accident. (Thanks, Dad!)

And that's why I always recommend to guys that they watch stand-up comedy, especially comedians that are great at one-liners and crowd work. If you watch five to ten minutes a day of these guys for a few months, it'll start to seep into the way you talk and interact with people in the best way possible.

Here's a few excellent comedians for you to check out:

- **Mark Normand:** The king of witty banter. He's got a one-liner for everything and is great at finding humor in everyday situations.
- **Sam Morrill:** He's known for his sharp wit and interesting commentary on dating, relationships, and the absurdities of modern life.

- **Bill Burr:** This guy is a great storyteller and can turn basically any subject into comedy gold.
- **Steven Wright:** He's renowned for his deadpan delivery and offbeat humor, along with some awesome one-liners.
- **Mitch Hedberg:** His laid-back demeanor and quirky one-liners can inspire you to bring a relaxed, playful energy to your flirting.
- **Andrew Schulz:** He has a boulder, boundary-pushing kind of comedic style. He's also got some amazing back-and-forths when he does crowd work, which can help strengthen your wit.

And, of course, if you want to try your own hand at stand-up comedy, that can be even better! There's plenty of open-mic nights in most big cities. If you're feeling up for the challenge, write down a quick five, get up there, and try it out for yourself.

Aside from stand-up comedy, improv can also be incredibly helpful with your wit and communication skills.

Essentially, improv is a form of live performance in which you create scenes, dialogues, and characters spontaneously and without a script. It's really easy to get into, and you can find affordable improv classes in any sizable city. I actually took improv classes early on in my dating journey and it made a big impact. Also, the nice bonus is that the classes are typically mostly women, and so you might even meet your next date there.

The really great thing about improv is that it forces you to think on your feet, release your fear of judgment, and adapt quickly to whatever is thrown your way—all key aspects of being great at flirting.

Raw Skills You'll Improve with Stand-Up Comedy & Improv:

- Quick wit
- Sense of humor
- Storytelling
- Self-amusement
- Reduced self-monitoring
- Spontaneity

Freestyle Rapping & Word Association

I know that this one might sound a little ridiculous, but humor me—I promise that you'll thank me later when you're flirting like a pro.

Picture this for a second. You walk on stage in front of thousands of people—the beat is bumping, the crowd is watching, and it's your turn to step up. You've got no script and no safety net—just your wit, your words, and your rhythm.

This is the exact situation I found myself in back in the fall of 2012. My friends had put on a Big Sean concert in Connecticut, and I was backstage helping with the set up. Big Sean was one of the biggest up and coming rappers at the time. I'd developed some rapping chops in college, and so it was cool to see the whole spectacle. And then, out of nowhere:

"Hey, bro—one of the opening acts just backed out. We need a few rappers to go up and freestyle for a few minutes," my friend told me.

"If you're asking me, I'm in," I replied. I had zero doubt that I could pull this off. Within 20 minutes, I was on stage with a few other rappers in front of thousands of Big Sean fans. I grabbed the mic, the beat dropped, and I let it flow.

"I do this with a passion…fire-breathing dragon. They said it was a dream, I said I'd make it happen," I rapped.

And just like that…a star was born. (I'm kidding, obviously.)

I nervously muttered my way through the rest of the freestyle and made it work, but it certainly wasn't anything special. The crowd wasn't exactly blown away. But the point remains:

Number one, whenever you have the chance to do something epic, take it. Even if you screw it up, you'll have a good story to tell. This includes going up and talking to that beautiful girl.

Number two, freestyle rap is something that every man should learn to do. Why? Well, what if I told you that the very skills you hone with freestyle rap can transform your everyday conversations, particularly in the realm of flirting and social interactions?

Funnily enough, this was something I realized early on as well, and it was another thing that helped me greatly accelerate my communication with women. I'd grown up listening to stand-up comedy and had spent years honing my craft at freestyle rap. And so a talent for wit came naturally.

And it's not just me. Let's look at the findings of a study titled "Neural Correlates of Lyrical Improvisation: An fMRI Study of Freestyle Rap," conducted by Siyuan Liu et al. and published in *Scientific Reports* in 2012.

Study Overview:

Objective: To examine the neural correlates of improvised, creative verbal expression (in this case, freestyle rap).

Participants: The study involved skilled freestyle rap artists who had substantial experience in improvisational performance.

What They Found:

Altered Brain Activity: The most striking finding was that freestyle rapping led to a unique pattern of brain activity. Specifically, increased activity in regions associated with emotion, language, motivation (such as the amygdala, prefrontal cortex, and language areas like Broca's area) and a decrease in regions linked with executive functions (like the dorsolateral prefrontal cortex), which are responsible for controlling behavior and decision making.

"Flow" State: The decreased activity in executive parts of the brain is particularly interesting. It suggests that when rappers are freestyling, they might be in a "flow" state, in which self-monitoring and deliberative thought processes are reduced, allowing for more spontaneous and fluid verbal generation. This is specifically interesting for you. The decrease in activity in executive regions of the brain could be likened to reducing the "filter" in everyday conversation, which allows for more natural, spontaneous interactions—as well as better flirting.

Enhanced Language and Emotional Expressivity: Increased activity in language and emotional regions of the brain indicates that freestyle rap enhances one's ability to access and use a rich vocabulary, as well as to express emotions more effectively. In flirting, this translates to being able to play with words more skillfully and convey feelings and attraction more compellingly.

Quick Thinking and Adaptability: The improvisational nature of freestyle rap trains the brain to think quickly and adapt. When flirting, this skill helps you to respond swiftly to conversational cues, keep up with the dynamic flow of the interaction, and even turn potentially awkward moments into opportunities for humor or deeper connection.

What All This Means for You:

Basically, you should add freestyle rap into your arsenal. Even just five minutes a day while driving to work or when you're hanging at home alone can make a big difference. Throw on an instrumental beat from YouTube and just let it flow. You can even use a word generator website or app to help you come up with topics. The more you do this, the less you'll run out of things to say and struggle to keep up with a woman's wit.

Raw Skills You'll Improve with Freestyle Rapping & Word Association:

- Quick wit
- Self-amusement
- Reduced self-monitoring
- Presence
- Spontaneity
- Storytelling
- Self-acceptance

Dance Classes

Every man should have at least a few dances moves up his sleeve.

Bachata, salsa, and country dancing are all solid options. Reggaeton is also great to learn if you want to get a little spicy with it.

These are all easy to learn with some beginner's dance classes. And what's great about dance classes is, like improv, they usually have more women than men, and so you'll likely meet some potential partners there, too.

Now, I'll stress here that I'm *far* from a dance expert. I've got four or five salsa and bachata moves that I can break out, but that's been enough for me to use on dates and at dance clubs. And it's especially helpful if you've got a thing for Latin women.

The point isn't to be a dance expert, though—it's more about the benefits of what a little bit of dancing can do for you.

It requires complete and immersive focus—you've got to be fully present in the moment. Dancing also helps you to connect with a woman not just physically but also emotionally, and so you're able to get more in tune with reading her cues.

It makes you better at leading, too. It's always the man's job to lead on the dance floor, just as it's his job to lead the conversations and dates. Dancing teaches you how to lead with assertiveness and empathy.

And as an added bonus, you can use dancing as a way to move things back to your place or hers. You can say, "Let's get out of here. I'd love to show you some of those dance moves we talked about." Or, once you're back home, you can show her a few bachata moves, which makes the mood intimate and provides an excuse to get physical.

Raw Skills You'll Improve with Dance Classes:

- Reduced self-monitoring
- Presence
- Spontaneity
- Self-acceptance
- Leading
- Empathy

Sitting in Silence

We live in a high-stimulation world. At any given moment, you can scroll on X, watch a TikTok video, listen to a podcast, swipe on a dating app—or even do them all at once!

With so many options at your fingertips, it's easy to never "shut things off" and to rarely have time to yourself.

That's the power of sitting in silence. This could be five or ten minutes a day in which you meditate or just focus on your breathing. There are plenty of apps like Calm and Headspace that can help you with this. Or you can just toss on some meditation or breathing music and relax.

Sitting in silence will help you become more present and get you comfortable with "just being," and this calm presence is key to effective flirting. It can also allow you to self-reflect, and the time spent away from your screen can help reduce anxiety. That way, you can become cool, calm, and collected during decisive moments of flirting.

A variation of this is simply going on meditative walks. Just walk through a nice area or park with some meditative music—you'll get some daily steps in, and you might also have some opportunities to approach cute girls along the way.

Raw Skills You'll Improve with Sitting in Silence:

- Presence
- Self-acceptance
- Empathy

Reading Fiction & Non-Fiction

At first, you may not connect the act of reading with your ability to flirt, but there's actually quite a bit of overlap.

For example, reading fiction helps improve your emotional intelligence, as it develops greater empathy and understanding of human emotions. It also broadens your imagination, which can help you have more engaging and creative conversations. It can expand your worldview, too, and make you a more intriguing and knowledgeable conversationalist.

Plus, it'll enable you to craft just the right dig when she tells you that she loved reading Harry Potter when she was younger.

Non-fiction, on the other hand, helps you to self-improve, informs you on a wide range of topics, and helps add more depth and substance to your personality.

You can add a daily reading habit of ten to fifteen minutes into your routine, mixing in both fiction and non-fiction books. I recommend reading non-fiction in the morning, as it can give you some ideas to ponder and take action on throughout your day. Fiction is best at night, as it's not too dense and can even help you fall asleep.

Raw Skills You'll Improve with Reading Fiction & Non-Fiction:

- Quick wit
- Self-amusement
- Self-acceptance
- Storytelling
- Empathy

Going for the Close

You need to get into the habit of leading things to the next step with women. This could mean inviting her to the next venue, inviting her home, or respectfully going for intimacy once you're in a private location like your place or hers.

When you've employed the flirting techniques we've uncovered in this book, you'll attract women and be able to do so quite quickly. And you may be surprised at just how often women will want to take the next step with you—as long as you have the courage to ask for it.

One thing to keep in mind is that attraction has a window, and so you've got to act quickly once you have it. If you wait too long and miss your chance, you probably won't get another.

Raw Skills You'll Improve with Going for the Close:

- Leading
- Self-acceptance
- Spontaneity
- Reduced self-monitoring

Consistent Action

Being consistent with all these activities will help you become a master at flirting, but you've also got to take consistent action in *all* aspects of dating:

- Getting premium photos for your dating profile so that you get more matches and dates
- Optimizing your Instagram so that you can convert more women from online dating and in-person approaches into first dates
- Starting conversations with women you find attractive in your day-to-day life

- Reflecting on what you can improve upon with each approach, conversation, and rejection

- Not giving up or settling when things feel a little bit difficult

Raw Skills You'll Improve with Consistent Action:

- All skills!

Key Takeaways

- **Leverage Stand-Up Comedy and Improv:** These can enhance many of your raw flirting skills like quick wit, sense of humor, and spontaneity.

- **Freestyle Rap for Quick Thinking:** It'll train you to think on your feet and reduce self-monitoring. Plus, it can help you to never run out of things to say.

- **Develop Your Rhythm with Dance Classes:** Dance forms like salsa, bachata, and country can boost your confidence and help improve your presence, leading, and empathy when you flirt.

- **Sit in Silence:** Enhancing your presence and focus by sitting in silence or meditative walking—these can reduce anxiety and help you to be "in the moment" when you flirt.

- **Read Fiction and Non-Fiction:** Reading expands your emotional intelligence, as well as boosts your creativity, empathy, and conversation skills. It also makes you a better storyteller.

- **Go for the Close:** Confidently lead interactions toward the next step. Whether you move to a new venue or escalate to intimacy, timely action is key before the window of attraction closes.

- **Take Consistent Action:** Take action on the activities here along with everything else you've learned in this book. Optimize your dating profile and IG, approach women in your day-to-day life, and learn from each interaction.

Final Thoughts

There are certain things in life that, once we do them, change us and we're never the same again. We forever stretch the limitations of what we initially thought was possible—climbing a mountain, running a marathon, skydiving, and I'm sure that you can think of a few others.

Improving our interactions with women and flirting belong in that category, too. I often call it the "gateway drug" to success in life.

There are so many men who spend their entire lives working on adjacent things, thinking that this will fix their dating life. They work on their finances, physique, career, appearance, and so on, only to then realize that all those things won't get them the kind of woman they want. To do that, they need to attack their dating life head on—with all the fears and insecurities that come along with it—and actually develop the communication skills that their dream woman craves in a man.

And once they decide to do this with intention, incredible changes can happen. They're fully at the helm now, and with more control than they've ever had before.

There's something magical about being able to walk up to a beautiful woman, get a conversation going, and know that you have a relatively good chance of attracting her. And if you can do that, what other incredible things are you capable of?

For myself and many of my clients, once we gained that ability and realization, we began to want more and more out of life. The idea of settling—something that may have once appealed to us in certain ways—no longer seems fulfilling.

The only way forward is to approach life in a full state of attack mode. You want something? Act in spite of your excuses and go for it. Something doesn't go your way? Take responsibility, make the necessary changes, and keep moving forward. There is no final failure—and no stopping until success is achieved.

And if you take this approach seriously, you'll open a door that most men never even have the courage to approach. You step into a world in which your full potential is on the table.

And that's kind of the point, isn't it?

You've only got one shot at this life, so there's no need to hold back.

Key Takeaways of the Book

The main takeaway within these pages is that flirting is a learnable skill. It's not some kind of a magic "secret sauce" that only a few men are blessed with.

Take what's in these pages and use it to develop your skills, and I promise that you'll exponentially improve your dating life.

I've emphasized what flirting is and how to see it from the woman's perspective. You've learned how to meet beautiful women in different environments, how to apply flirting techniques in different situations, and how to become a natural at flirting through building the right raw skills.

You're now equipped with everything you need to get out there and have amazing conversations with women—conversations that'll get them attracted and keep them coming back for more.

Use your newfound skills wisely—remember to always have genuinely good intentions when you interact with women. They'll feel the love, kindness, and warmth behind your words, and become comfortable relaxing and showing you their "secret side" that they so rarely expose to men.

And that, my friends, is a magical thing.

Need Some Extra Help?

We've reached the end of Book 1, and if you like what you've read so far, you'll love my podcast—***Dating Decoded***.

I wanted a platform where I could give you plenty of awesome, unfiltered dating tips and advice to help you immediately improve your game, score more dates, and get closer to meeting your dream partner.

You can check out a popular episode here:

Dating Decoded Episode 29: What To Do When You're Scared To Talk To Girls

Just search "Dating Decoded" on your favorite podcast platform or navigate to: https://spoti.fi/44xbuRn

You'll discover simpler strategies you can use to instantly overcome the fear of approaching an attractive girl--and feel ten times more confident.

Now, let's move on to book 2!

Book 2

Conversation Casanova (The New & Improved Edition)

How to Effortlessly Start Conversations, Make Deep Connections & Attract Women

Prologue: Straight Talk

"How Does He Make It Look So Easy?"

It's a scenario that I'm willing to bet you're fairly familiar with. You're out at the bar and see an ordinary, normal-looking guy approaching a beautiful woman. Within minutes, she's completely enraptured by the conversation. Laughing, smiling, touching the guy...the whole nine yards.

All the while, you sit back and wonder what kind of magic spell he's put her under (and also wondering why *you* didn't go up and talk to her first!).

"Is he rich? Were they friends beforehand? Are they dating? What's he saying to her? How does he make it look so easy?" Your brain is on overload trying to figure out this guy's magic touch.

Before you know it, she's putting her number into his phone—and then she's leaving the bar with him!

You're suddenly slammed with feelings of jealousy and envy. You think back to all your conversations with women in which you couldn't find the right word or just "click" with them—or worse, in which you didn't even have the courage to talk to her in the first place!

This kind of thing used to happen to me *all the time*. And if you're reading this book, I'm guessing that it's happened to you, too.

So what are these guys saying? How are they connecting, flirting, and attracting women so quickly and effortlessly?

Well, what you're about to discover in this book is that it's not that complicated after all.

The guys who "get it" all do similar things in their conversation. They know how to flirt, connect, and make women laugh.

What's more, you'll also discover a system so that you can easily replicate these types of conversations—*and* add your own style.

Sounds great, right?

But just hang on for a minute.

You might be thinking, "What about all those studies saying that 95% of communication is non-verbal? Is conversation really *that* important?"

Fair point. But answer me this: If you try to watch a movie in a different language without subtitles, will you understand 95% of it?

Certainly not. (And trust me, I've tried.)

Sure, there are a lot of things that you can (and should) communicate non-verbally, and we'll go over them in-depth in this book.

But in order to *truly* connect with a woman, you need to use your words.

This is how you discover her deeper aspirations, her personality, and whether or not she's a good fit for you.

It's *how* you'll ask her certain questions that'll give the interaction a deeper meaning.

What's more, this is how you make her *feel* something. And if you can make a woman feel amazing, she can't help but be attracted to you.

Plus, the more you can connect with people through conversation, the more your world will open up to you in general.

Soon, you won't have to wonder how those guys make it "look so easy"—because *you'll* be the guy who the other guys look at with jealousy as you effortlessly attract women with your words.

Your dating life will be abundant, your relationships will flourish, and you'll have more opportunities than you can imagine.

So just how do you master conversation, connect with women, and harness the power of your words?

This book has all those answers and more. It outlines a system that anyone can use to unlock the power of conversation.

Whether you're talking to women during the daytime, at the bar in the evening, or at a social event, it doesn't matter. This conversation system will work anywhere and at any time.

So get ready and buckle up. The way you talk to people—and, more specifically, women—is about to change forever.

How to Master Conversation

This book is divided into six key parts:

1. **The Casanova Mindsets:** Mastering the frames of mind that are essential for attracting women
2. **Become a Top-Tier Man:** Build your "girl-getting machine" and have the courage to talk to anyone
3. **Initiate the Conversation:** How to approach a woman and get the conversation going
4. **Connect:** How to develop the conversation and truly mesh with women
5. **Captivate:** Compel and attract women through your conversation skills
6. **Relationships, Compatibility, and Maintaining the Masculine Frame:** How to tell if she's the right woman for you and build the relationship the right way

Part 1 gives you the mindset of a man who attracts women through conversation. This will be your foundation.

Part 2 helps you create an attitude and persona that'll makes it easy for you to get dates. It'll also show you how to destroy your anxiety about starting conversations so that you can approach that pretty girl with ease.

Part 3 is your guide to getting the conversation started. You'll discover easy ways to initiate conversations in different environments, along with how to build the conversation from there.

Part 4 shows you how to truly connect with women. You'll discover what to do and what *not* to do so that your conversations flow smoothly and you can engage with women easily.

Part 5 teaches you to capture women's attention and attract them through your conversational charisma. You'll learn how to hook her in with stories and how to talk about yourself in an appealing way.

And finally, **Part 6** provides you with the next steps after you've established a connection. You'll learn how to build things from the first date all the way to a healthy relationship, how to tell if she's a good fit for you (or not), and maintain a masculine frame so that you can keep her attracted for the long haul.

Now, let's dive right into Part 1: The Casanova Mindsets That Drive Her Wild.

Part 1: The Casanova Mindsets That Drive Her Wild

"Once your mindset changes, everything on the outside will change along with it."

— Steve Maraboli, bestselling author and motivational speaker

Why Your Mindsets Are Crucial

Think of your mindsets as your foundation.

With a solid foundation, you can build something sturdy and strong, right?

But with a shaky foundation, you have a house of cards. If one little thing goes wrong, it can send the whole thing toppling down—and bring *you* along with it.

Adding to that, a solid mindset will generally help you take the right course of action. Even if you've never faced a particular situation before, you'll be able to react calmly and efficiently, even if it might seem daunting.

On the opposite end, a poor mindset can cause you to freak out and react negatively. And I see this all the time with guys I work with—the ones who stumble and fumble with their sour outlook compared to the ones who can let not-very-ideal circumstances roll right off their back. These guys make the fastest improvements and aren't bogged down by constant emotional swings.

So it should come as no surprise that your mindset is *especially* important when it comes to dating and conversation.

For example, let's say that you've hung out with a girl a few times. Things seem to be going well—you have fun together and you seem to connect with each other easily.

But maybe you've unconsciously adopted a negative mindset, such as "I need women to prove my self-worth."

So when she doesn't text you back for a day, your mind starts flooding with insecurity. "Has she figured me out? I *knew* that I wasn't good enough after all! Wait, who does this girl think she is? I'll show her!" Then you lash out and tell her that you deserve better and you can't believe that she's being so inconsiderate.

She explains that she was studying for a test, and she can't believe that you're so rude. And guess what? That's the last you'll hear from her.

See, if you have a bad mindset, it doesn't matter how successful you are with women. The second you get a negative signal from a girl, it can trigger a downward spiral. That's because your confidence and self-worth will be dependent on her approval.

But with a positive mindset, you can brush things off more easily and move on. And what's more, you'll be far more likely to say the right things in conversation.

For example, if you have a positive mindset, like "All women are attracted to me until proven otherwise," you'll talk to a woman like she's actually attracted to you (and she probably will be). In doing so, you'll be more flirtatious and confident—and also far more likely to move the conversation toward what you want (like future dates or meet-ups).

Remember: Your mindsets dictate your thoughts, your thoughts dictate your actions, and your actions dictate your results.

Part I is all about diving into the Casanova mindsets for conversation. Once you internalize these foundations, everything else will become much easier.

So follow along closely, put the action steps into action, and get ready for a mental shift.

Taking Responsibility for Your Life

Sad but true: The average guy won't have the success that he craves with women.

Instead, odds are that his dating trajectory will look something like this:

- He'll meet a few girls through his friends and college classes, dating a few here and there.
- When he graduates, he'll meet a girl or two from his work.
- Occasionally, he might go out, get drunk, and "get lucky" with a new girl at the bar or club...usually one who's below his standards.
- He'll get tired of the single life and start dating a girl from his social circle, or maybe even an average-enough girl from a dating app (albeit one who he's not very excited about), more so out of scarcity than actually seeing a future with her—after all, he has minimal dating options. The relationship will go on a little longer than it probably should.
- This cycle will continue until he eventually settles with and marries a woman who he thinks is "the best he can do," though she doesn't really match up with his values or have the traits that he desires.
- He'll bicker with his friends about how his wife is always trying to "control" him and take his freedom, and this will go on and on for years.
- Divorce, death, taxes, etc.

It seems bleak, I know. But there's a reason why the divorce rate is above 50% in the USA and why more and more men are single and alone than ever before (nearly one in three young men, according to one study [1]).

In short, the guy illustrated above doesn't have much control over his dating life—or his life in general. He's highly dependent on the girls who "stumble" into his life through work, friends, and drunken escapades.

The good news? This guy doesn't have to be you. You can break the cycle.

But here's the thing: If you don't take control of your life, it's impossible to get what you want.

Your results will be random, and you will not be happy with that randomness.

So if you've ever, at some point, considered leaving your "dating life up to chance," remember the above.

Also, if you haven't left your career, finances, or other important things in your life up to chance, then why would you choose to do so with your relationships? The person you spend the rest of your life with will greatly impact every one of those other areas and your overall fulfillment in life. Do you want that to be something that you "hope works out" or something that you're intentional about?

Casanova Mindset #1: I am responsible for my life and my circumstances.

Think back to your failures with women (hey, we've all had them). There was always a *reason* for those failures. Sometimes you had control of the outcome, and sometimes you didn't. But you have to remove the blame from the women and take full responsibility.

For example:

- You're on a date with a girl and the conversation is flowing. You tell her about your proudest accomplishments and hint at how much money you make. She smiles and nods but doesn't text you back after the date. And of course not—she can sense the insecurity. **Why would she want a man who feels the need to constantly impress her?**

- You become infatuated with a girl you're dating. You think about her all the time and heap your affection on her whenever you can. She seems happy at first but then quickly becomes more and more distant. Eventually, she backs off and asks for some time apart. **Why would she want a man who makes a woman his main purpose?**

These are situations in which you'd be tempted to become bitter toward women. But instead, you need to manage your emotions, shift your perspective, and accept responsibility. By taking ownership of the problem, you can focus on what you need to improve instead of becoming bitter.

Think of how this mindset will affect your conversations. With it, you'll understand that you're responsible for:

- Making something happen with her
- Leading the conversation in a positive way
- The outcome of the interaction

In understanding these things, you'll shift the way you look at conversation—and you'll be far more likely to take action on the nitty-gritty conversation tactics we'll explore in this book.

Also, think about how this mindset can affect your life in a larger sense.

See, most people live reactive lives—they're victims of their circumstances and react to whatever life throws at them. But to be successful in any area, you must take success into your own hands. You need to realize that you have much more control over your circumstances and your life than you might think.

Key Takeaways:

- **Own Up:** When you don't take ownership of your life and "leave things to chance," you're much more likely to get unfavorable results.
- **Be Intentional:** Attack what's important to you head on, and don't leave room for any excuses.
- **Take 100% Responsibility:** It doesn't matter what cards you were dealt—it's your responsibility to turn it into a great hand and create a life that you're excited about.

Action Tip: Write down two things in your life that you feel like you're not taking full responsibility for. After that, write down how you can take control of these things right now.

For example: "I've put on some weight because I haven't been going to the gym. I can take control of this by finding a gym routine and sticking to it 3 times a week."

Resources:

1. Ueda P, Mercer CH, Ghaznavi C, Herbenick D. Trends in Frequency of Activity and Number of Partners Among Adults Aged 18 to 44 Years in the US, 2000-2018. JAMA Netw Open. 2020;3(6):e203833. doi:10.1001/jamanetworkopen.2020.3833

Overcoming the Need for Validation

Deep down, most men believe that they're inherently "not enough." They need other things to complete them—women, money, fame, a great physique, and so on (or some combination of all those things).

They want to be respected by other men and desired by attractive women, but this leads to needy behavior because they're always trying to find the "missing piece." It makes their conversations shallow because they always aim to "get something" out of the other person.

But here's the thing: You'll *never* find that missing piece. There will always be more to desire.

Once you score a date with a girl, you'll want to bring her back to your place. Once you achieve that, you'll want to get intimate with her. Then you'll want to tell your friends about it and "show her off." That'll be nice and feel good, but that good feeling will wear off.

Soon, you'll want more. You'll want to experience this feeling of approval again, and you'll need other women to fill that need. You'll have to keep trying harder to impress your friends and your parents. The cycle will never end.

If you're thinking, "I don't have this problem!", I have a question for you.

Think of what it'll be like to date or pick up your dream girl. What excites you more? The thought of experiencing her beauty, personality, and passion? Or bragging to your friends about getting such a "hottie?"

Be honest with yourself.

For a long time, it was the latter for me. I approached and talked to women largely to impress other men. It was the only way I could prove my worth.

I remember when I started college and pledged a fraternity. At that point, I had only been intimate with one girl, while all the other fraternity guys bragged about having been with ten or more. I felt like I wasn't enough. I needed more.

So I made it a point to become intimate with as many women as possible—and also brag about it as much as I could. I often came off shallow though, because women could tell that I didn't care about *them*—I only wanted the validation they'd give me and to put another notch into my belt.

But now I have a much different perspective. When I see a woman, I don't think of the validation she can give me. Instead, I think, "She's attractive and I want to meet her. I'll find out if she's cool, and if she is, maybe we can make something happen."

So, for you, the question is how do you overcome the need for validation?

This leads us to our second mindset.

Casanova Mindset #2: I am enough. I don't need the approval of anyone else to feel complete.

Many people live their lives in default mode, meaning that they don't take the time to analyze their true motivations and desires.

Oftentimes, their motivations are based on getting approval from other people. For me—and maybe for you, too—this was always the case. In doing so, we focus on living up to other people's values instead of our own. That's a recipe for failure because we never figure out and execute on things that are important to us.

Two of my biggest values are freedom and creativity. Back when I was studying accounting in university, I focused on living up to my parents' values of security and stability. This, predictably, led to extreme unhappiness and stress.

But when I started focusing more on my values, I became much happier. Now I enjoy the freedom I have to travel, as well as the creativity I can harness to make videos and write books like this one.

When you focus on getting approval, you live up to other people's values. But when you develop the mindset that "you are enough," you start living up to your own values—and that makes you unstoppable.

Key Takeaways:

- **No Need for Validation:** Most people live their lives to impress others instead of doing what they actually want. This is counterproductive and leads to unhappiness.
- **Reflect on Your Values:** Doing so will help you live a life more aligned with your own principles and needs rather than those of others.
- **Adopt the "I Am Enough" Mindset:** Stop looking for approval from others to feel complete—the only "thumbs up" you need is your own.

Action Tip: Write down your five most important values, rating yourself from 1 to 10 for each. For the ones that you rate poorly, think of how you can improve upon them and write down how.

For example, let's say that you value freedom and wealth, but you're working at a time-consuming job that doesn't pay well. Maybe this means that you should start a side hustle of some kind so that you can eventually quit your job, achieve more freedom, and make more money.

A Man With Purpose

We've all heard some kind of variation of the quote, "If you don't know where you're going, you might end up someplace else."

Most men don't know where they're going. They're so focused on making a living that they forget to actually *live*. This purposeless existence is terrible for building a life and even more terrible for dating.

Women are attracted to men with purpose, a driving goal that propels them forward despite the obstacles. And men with a purpose don't depend on women's approval.

They also aren't affected by a bad conversation or two.

Women know when they're talking to men with purpose because these men have a different kind of look in their eyes. They *know* where they're going—they have an edge. They strive for something instead of "going with the flow" and simply drifting in the wind.

Casanova Mindset #3: Women are *not* my #1 priority. I have a mission and purpose outside of chasing them down.

You need to have a mission in life other than being on a constant conquest for women. Otherwise, you'll be too tempted to give up on your passions and your direction in life and focus completely on finding a mate (or, even worse for the long term, nothing more than a fling). Women will sense that they're the center of your world, and you won't be able to genuinely love them or connect with them. Instead, you'll rely on them to fill needs that they cannot fill. This will undermine your conversations and your relationships.

However, understand that you can have multiple priorities.

If you mostly ignore women to focus on your purpose, you'll stifle yourself socially (not to mention be incredibly lonely). Then, when you've achieved your goals and it is time to date, you may actually have a harder time with it.

This is for two reasons. First, you'll have more to lose in terms of finances, reputation, the life you've built, and so on. Second, you may not have the social acumen and awareness to protect yourself from bad players, like women who may want you for the wrong reasons (such as your wealth instead of your character), or to spot red flags that could lead to unhealthy relationships.

While it's possible to have success regardless—and plenty of men do—it's a lot easier to save time for social skills and dating while you're "on the way up" than when you're already there and have delayed it for years.

That being said, if you're already "on the top," the best time to focus on this is today.

Key Takeaways:

- **Set Goals and Strive for Them:** Refuse to "drift"—instead, attack your life with a purpose.
- **Don't Make Women Your #1 Priority:** Have a mission in life outside of women, but don't ignore dating altogether, as it'll stunt your growth overall.

Action Tip: Find your purpose. Ask yourself, *"What was a moment when I felt extremely energized and excited? What was I doing at that time?"* Write down your answer. By recognizing what makes you feel most alive and invigorated, you can better understand your motivations. This can help you clarify your purpose.

Thinking back to my early days, I always loved to write, and I'd post multiple social media blogs every week. I also loved to be in front of large groups of people—I'd perform rap songs every chance I could.

Now, through my books, videos, and coaching, I have the privilege of doing both (though I've taken it easy on the rap career).

So dig deep with this action tip and ask yourself how you can start doing more of the things that make you come alive. By pursuing these passions, you'll give yourself the best chance to create a life that you're truly proud of.

She's Into Me

Most women aren't going to come straight out and tell you that they like you. This poses a problem for most guys, especially if they're on the beginner end of the spectrum.

You spend your time searching for signs that a woman is attracted to you, but all the while, you don't really understand how to read those signs.

The result? You move slower with women as you struggle to decode. And when you don't get the signs you think you need, you avoid making a move, thereby losing your chance with her.

But there's a solution to this. It's a mighty and bold move, but trust me on it:

You should assume attraction from all women until proven otherwise. And by "proven otherwise," I mean until she literally walks away or flat-out tells you that she isn't interested.

However, you obviously need to be smart about this. Don't cross the line and make women uncomfortable with unwanted physical advances. If she says no or is clearly disinterested, then halt your advances.

Casanova Mindset #4: All women are attracted to me until proven otherwise.

This is the frame of mind you need to adapt:

Is she dressed nicely? It's because she's trying to impress you. She's playing with her hair? She's into you. Is she presenting herself with solid posture? It's because she wants you to notice her figure.

You need to assume that every single sign she gives you is a green flag of her attraction and interest.

Compare this to the "innocent until proven guilty" nice guy approach. This guy writes off *all* those signs. For example: "Oh, she's playing with her hair? She must just be adjusting it" or "She made eye contact with me? It must have been an accident."

You must take the first approach. When you see and interact with women you're interested in, you need to act as if you're going to date them and that there's the potential to get intimate.

This will change the way you talk to women, and it'll also allow you to meet more of them.

Think of all the ways this mindset can come in handy:

- See that pretty girl sitting in the café? Assume that she'll be attracted to you and go introduce yourself.
- You're out on a date? Assume that she wants to go home with you, so ask if she wants to go back to your place for a drink.
- Texting a girl and trying and score a date? Assume that she's already interested and just ask her out.

By assuming attraction, you'll give yourself the best chance with women in every interaction.

Now, a disclaimer: Assuming attraction won't make women magically fall all over you. If a girl isn't interested in you, simply "assuming attraction" won't be enough to win her over.

But if you approach them confidently, most women will be at least a little intrigued and more open to you. By assuming attraction, you'll filter out the women who wouldn't have been into you anyway and give yourself a much better chance of attracting the women who might be interested.

What's crazy here is that your reality starts to reflect your beliefs. When you assume that women are attracted to you, you'll start acting like it. You'll make more innuendos, lead women, and put yourself in a position to succeed. You'll be more comfortable interacting with women because you won't be worried about picking up on their signs of attraction.

Key Takeaways:

- **Assume Her Attraction From the Start:** Take every sign that she gives you as one of attraction and interest. This gives you confidence and helps you to move things forward.
- **Know When to Dial It Back:** Be smart about things if she shows signs of disinterest. If she's clearly not into you, either let it go or aim to flirt and connect more to get her invested in the interaction.

Action Tip: Write down two thoughts that come to mind when you see a girl you're attracted to. Ask yourself: Are these thoughts empowering?

Action Tip 2: When you see a girl, imagine her responding very positively toward you. Then say to yourself, "This girl wants to meet me."

This mindset will help you approach and lead women, make the move, and improve pretty much every other aspect of your dating life. It'll also give you a big shot of confidence.

5 More Key Mindsets To Crush It On Your Dating Journey

Let's examine some other key mindsets that'll make you a more attractive man, as well as make the journey to improving your game with women much easier.

These mindsets, which I've constructed after coaching thousands of guys, will help you overcome the pitfalls you're likely to face at some point on your journey if you truly want to master the dating skillset.

1. There's Always Another One Coming

All too often, guys will "fall hard" for a girl almost right away. They'll seemingly forget about every other girl in the world and become hyper-fixated on *this* one.

In my early days, we'd jokingly call this "cherish mode," in which the guy overanalyzes every text message, date, and interaction with her.

It's great to meet a girl you click with, but be careful about falling into the headspace that "there's no other girl like her."

The moment you start acting like a relationship is your only chance at happiness, you lose your edge. You become clingy, desperate, and full of anxiety—and no one wants to be around that energy. But when you know that there's always another girl coming, you can relax, take things slow, and let connections develop naturally without forcing anything.

You need to command the attitude of, "If it works out with this girl, great! If not, there'll be another one around the corner."

The one caveat: This doesn't mean that you're "going with the flow." Instead, it assumes that you're taking consistent action to bring more of these women into your life. So keep your foot on the gas pedal!

The more dating success you have, the easier it'll be to adapt this mindset because you'll see it playing out in real time.

2. Be Careful Who You Listen To

One of the biggest traps in life—and especially in dating—is taking advice from people who haven't achieved what you want or who can't even relate to your journey.

It's tempting to seek guidance from parents, teachers, or friends—after all, they're often the closest people to us. But if they're not where you want to be or their values and goals don't align with yours, their advice can lead you astray.

Parents, for instance, might offer advice based on their experiences, but they're likely from a different generation with different norms and expectations. They might push you toward safety and stability, focusing on what worked for them 30 years ago. The dating game has changed drastically since then, and what made sense in their time could leave you spinning your wheels in today's world. What helped your dad attract Susie from the local neighborhood probably won't work when you want to attract that pretty girl walking down the street in a big city.

Instead, listen to people who've achieved what you're striving for. Seek out mentors, coaches, or friends who embody the success that you want to achieve.

These people have walked the path you're on, faced the same challenges, and found a way to thrive. They can offer insights and shortcuts to success that others can't.

One additional note: If the people in your life don't think that your improvement journey is a little whacky, you're probably not going hard enough.

There were multiple times in my journey when my friends and family thought I was crazy for trying to blaze my own path. Now that I have the receipts and proved that it was right for me, they understand. But had I listened to them, my life would be a whole lot less fulfilling for *me*.

3. Try "Cringe-Level" Hard

If you want to achieve a level of success most guys only can dream of, it's going to be a bumpy road on the way up.

Trying "cringe-level" hard is about taking risks, making mistakes, and stumbling in front of everyone without caring about what they think. It's the mindset that says, "I'm doing whatever it takes to create the life that I want, even if it feels embarrassing."

When you're out there practicing your social skills, approaching women, and experimenting with new techniques, you'll have moments that make even *you* cringe. Maybe you fumble your words or the girl you approach isn't interested, or you make a total fool of yourself on the dance floor. These are the times when most guys would slink away in embarrassment, but you're not most guys, are you?

You try hard because you're not here to impress the peanut gallery—you're here to get results. And while others are playing it safe, you're out there learning from every misstep, gathering experiences, and building the resilience needed to succeed.

In the end, when you're standing on the other side with a beautiful girl on your arm and supercharged confidence, those same people who cringed at you will be asking how you did it. And it'll feel pretty damn amazing.

So don't worry about their opinions; worry instead about your results. In fact, don't "worry" about them—just try "cringe-level" hard and you'll find that the growth and success that follow are worth every awkward moment.

4. Even Keeled: Don't Get Too High Or Too Low

There's no way around it—you're going to face ups and downs on your journey.

There'll be times when you feel like "It's so over" and other times where you feel like "I'm so back!" When you're riding high on a wave of good results, it's natural to feel on top of the world. But the real trick is to not let that rush go to your head. You acknowledge the win and savor the moment, but you don't let success inflate your ego. Instead, you use it as a stepping stone, a checkpoint that lets you know that you're heading in the right direction.

I learned this lesson the hard way both in dating and in business. Back when I was a door-to-door sales guy, I broke the rookie record for sales in my first two weeks. I was riding high and thought that I was unstoppable.

But then I hit exactly $0 in sales the following week. I let my hubris get the best of me and I crashed right back down to Earth. And it felt all the more crushing because of the high I allowed myself to feel from the week before. So enjoy the wins, but stay grounded.

Conversely, when things take a nosedive—maybe a date didn't pan out or you hit a streak where it feels like nothing's working—you don't let despair take the wheel. Sure, you feel the sting, but you don't sink into it. Rather than getting bogged down in frustration or self-pity, you extract the lessons hidden within the setback.

Being even keeled doesn't mean that you're devoid of passion or that you don't care about outcomes—it means that you have mastery over your reactions.

You can celebrate the wins and learn from the losses, but you don't let either throw you off course. It's about taking it all in stride and keeping your focus on the bigger picture, knowing that success isn't just one big victory and defeat isn't a single rough patch—it's about how you keep moving through it all without losing your cool.

Remember: You're playing the long game here.

5. Fix the Problem By Fixing It!

As we examined in mindset #3 on mission and purpose, guys will focus on every other part of their life—money, fitness, style—in hopes that it'll somehow fix their dating life, too. It's the "Focus on yourself, king!" mindset that so many influencers in the "red pill" movement like to preach.

But here's the catch: Those things can only take you so far. You might look good on the outside, but if you haven't developed the dating skills—not being able to hold a conversation, handle rejection, or build chemistry—it won't matter how fit, rich, or stylish you are.

What's ironic is that many of my dating coaching clients come to me after they've achieved all that. They believed the lie that these things would fix everything in their dating life, too, but became confused when things didn't play out that way.

Here's the problem: The dating game is a competition, and you're competing against other men. And if you're reading this book, I'm guessing that you're not aiming to be in the bottom 80% to 90%—you're aiming to be in the top 10%. That way, you can have access to and attract the highest quality women.

And you better believe that the guys in that top 10% have done what it takes to excel in both dating and their careers, as well as those other areas.

So by "putting off" dating, you're giving yourself a handicap and allowing those other guys to lap you. Sure, you can catch up, but it's going to take a lot more work than if you hadn't avoided building your social and dating skills for years.

The way that you fix your dating life is by *fixing your dating life*.

You've got to face the uncomfortable stuff and do the things that scare you: talk to more women, risk rejection, and keep improving. That's how you *actually* fix the problem.

And if you want a glimpse into how the journey of improving with women might look for you, **check out this podcast episode of mine on Spotify: How to Actually Get Your Dating Life Handled.**

Key Takeaways:

- **There's Always Another One Coming:** If you meet an awesome girl, great! But don't rush to put all your eggs into one basket and believe that she's the only girl out there who can make you happy.
- **Careful Who You Listen To:** Be cautious about taking advice from people who haven't achieved what you're aiming for, or who want safety and security for you above all else.

- **Try "Cringe-Level" Hard:** You're not taking this journey to impress anyone—you're doing it to reach your full potential as a man. The road may be bumpy and you may not look amazing on the way up, but the doubters will see the results soon enough.
- **Don't Get Too High or Too Low:** Enjoy the wins and learn from the losses, but stay even keeled and keep the big picture in mind so that you can consistently improve.
- **Fix Your Dating Life by Addressing It:** There's no getting around doing the hard work. If you want awesome results in your dating life, you've got to address it head on and face your fears around it.

Part 2: Becoming a Top-Tier Man

Building a Premium Brand: Your "Girl-Getting Machine"

As I sit here updating this book for 2024 and beyond, I have no choice but to add a section on modern dating and how to operate within it.

See, there's a new dynamic at play that you must account for if you want to succeed: the rise of online dating and Instagram.

Even earlier than about a decade ago, you could just be another face in the crowd with just a little bit of charm and still attract high quality women. While that remains the case in some ways, you're at a massive disadvantage if that's *all* you do, and I'd be doing you a disservice if I didn't cover this new dynamic and show you how to master it as well.

With online dating and Instagram bigger than ever, every single man has a brand. Your brand is basically your online footprint—it's the way you represent yourself to the world. The better that footprint is, the less women will flake on you and the higher value you'll be perceived to have. And as you increase your value in the dating marketplace, you'll increase your access to the highest quality women.

The added benefit is that if you're a successful, busy guy, you may not have tons of time to approach a high volume of women on a week-to-week basis. Online dating and Instagram allow you to line up dates from the comfort of your own home and within your busy schedule. And for you guys who do have extra time to approach women, you can use online dating to supplement what you're already doing in person. Either way, it's the easiest "engine" out there for generating a high number of dates in a short amount of time, which can help accelerate you on the path to meeting your life partner.

Now, you can choose to ignore this whole dynamic at the risk of becoming the "old man yelling at clouds" meme, or you can accept the way society has moved, go with the flow, and use it to your advantage. If you want to choose the first option, there's no judgment here, but you probably won't need this chapter. For those of you opting for the second route, let's dive in.

What it Takes to Be a "Catch" in the Modern Dating Market

To build a premium brand, you need to know what's actually attractive in the dating market, so let's cover the key things you'll want to exude.

Communication Skills & Flirting Ability

This is still the biggest key of all, and you'll learn about it extensively in this book. You can have everything else, but if you don't have these capabilities, you'll struggle mightily.

You need to know how to act, what to talk about, and how to elicit emotions when you're in front of a woman. Otherwise, this whole brand you've built up will seem incongruent when she meets you and you won't get past the first date.

A "Looksmaxxed" Appearance

You don't need to be conventionally good looking, but you *do* need to look good, and every single man can achieve this.

When I say "looksmaxxed," I mean the following:

- **Hairstyle and Grooming:** You're cleaned up, have a hairstyle that matches the shape of your face, and are always well-groomed.
- **Clothing Style:** You wear clothes that fit well, show off your physique, and go well together.
- **Accessories:** You have at least one or two accessories that match your style, like a watch, bracelet, or chain.
- **Physique:** You go to the gym consistently (at least three times a week) and build muscle.

If you want to clean things up even further, you can go to an esthetician and see what else can be optimized—within reason. For example, most guys in their thirties and beyond could benefit from a little Botox, while other guys may want to look into getting a hair transplant.

Looksmaxxing will help you make better first impressions online and in person, as well as make your dating life significantly easier to build. And it's not hard to execute on all this—you can get the style and hair on point with one haircut and a quick shopping trip. Depending on where you are with your physique, you can usually get to where you want to be in less than six months and start attracting women *now* as you make those changes. Women will see that you're on the level-up game, respect it, and be attracted to you—even if you haven't hit your goal yet.

(As a side note, I've had several coaching clients who've weighed over 300 pounds who were able to attract women and get dates while working on their fitness goals.)

Premium Instagram

Once you've optimized your look and taken some stellar photos, it's time to show yourself off to the world. There are two elements to doing this: Instagram and dating profiles. We'll dig into Instagram first.

As a man, Instagram is basically your "dating resume." Women can find it if you link it to your dating profile or if you exchange it with them during an approach. Also, women are resourceful—even if they don't tell you about it, most will find your Instagram before a date and do their research. But if it's not put together well, your flake rate is going to be high and you'll miss lots of opportunities.

From looking at thousands of guys IGs over the years, I can promise you that 99% aren't just weak—they're also "instant rejection" material; if a girl sees it, the guy's immediately out (not to mention how a bad IG can affect career prospects, too). And if you're wondering if *yours* is up to par...well, if you haven't put the work in to intentionally get it on point, it's not.

A solid Instagram profile should have the following:

- **Main Photo:** A headshot in which you stand out clearly from the background.
- **Bio:** Three or four emojis with quick lines about yourself and what you do, along with a pin emoji for your current city.
- **Highlights Section:** Premium-looking highlights from your life.
- **Photos:** High-quality lifestyle, hobby, and friend shots. Between five and ten top-end pictures is a decent goal to aim for, and then build from there.
- **Captions:** Keep them fun and playful, with a little seriousness mixed in every now and then.

- **Follower Ratio:** 2/1 (or better).
- **Username:** Should be your name or as close to it as possible (make it *easy* and *simple* to type and read out).

If you can do all this, you'll instantly position yourself as a top 10% man and it'll become significantly easier for you to get dates.

I built a personal Instagram as an example of what this should look like, **so use it as a barometer:** https://www.instagram.com/david.john.official/.

Premium Dating Profiles

Similar to your Instagram, you need to represent yourself well on your dating profile.

Women have more options online, and the top 20% of men get the lion's share of the matches and dates. Luckily, the bottom 80% of men do next to nothing to brand themselves well, so it's quite easy to catapult yourself above them.

Here's how to go the extra mile:

- **High-Quality, Top-Shelf Photos:** This is by far the main deciding factor for women to swipe right or left on you. If you want to attract top-tier women, you can't use grainy photos, selfies, or just overall low-quality shots—you simply won't have a chance if you do.
- **Fun, Playful Bio and Prompts:** You should use these to show some of your personality and give her a glimpse of the fun she'll have when the two of you hang out. It's *not* a place to write a two-paragraph biography about yourself and exactly what you're looking for—that's a bottom 80% profile trait.

- **Solid poses, framing, and backgrounds:** You must have these on point with your photos to be in the top percentage of men. As for posing, your body must be positioned well. With framing, you should generally take up one-third of the frame. And for backgrounds, you should generally have outdoor photos with at least two or three city backgrounds mixed in (as these look more premium).

For some examples of what top-tier dating profile photos look like, you can see a bunch listed here (along with some things you'll want to avoid): https://www.instagram.com/beastphotos_official/.

A Mix of High Potential & Real Results in Your Life

You've got to have some substance to you. If you have everything mentioned above dialed in, sure—you'll be able to have short-term flings. But if you want to not just attract high-quality women but also keep them around, your life needs to be going somewhere. And honestly, you should do this for yourself more so than for the purpose of attracting women—it's one of those things that you should just have a handle on, and not be content living in your parent's basement forever.

For guys roughly 27 and below, you want to max out your "potential factor." Somebody on the outside should be able to look at your life and what you're doing and think, "This guy is going places."

You don't necessarily need to have hard and fast results just yet, but you should seem like you're on the path to getting there. For example, a guy studying in school to become a doctor is probably broke right now, but he sure won't be in a few years. It's similar to someone who just quit his job to start his own business. It's ideal at this point to have several plates spinning with the potential to really hit big.

Once you're above 27, you can't rely as much on potential anymore, and you've got to have some real results to back up what you're doing. That business you started should be generating some sort of revenue, and you shouldn't be living paycheck to paycheck. It's okay if you're not crushing it on all fronts, but the successes should at least start to come in at this point.

For example, I relied a lot on my potential early on in my twenties. I had very little to back up my aspirations, aside from a blog generating zero money and a little bit of traffic, as well as hopes of world travel. But I dated a lot of beautiful, successful women like doctors and lawyers. They saw the potential in me. Later on in my twenties when I started seeing success, I had more access to resources and was no longer intimidated by successful women—or really any type of women for that matter. And they appreciated and accepted me the same as when I was "just potential."

Now, you may be reading this and thinking, "My potential and results generated aren't in a good place right now. What should I do?" Fair question. The good news is that you can change this around quickly.

How to do this is a bit outside the scope of this book (I wrote another book on this topic called *The Lifestyle Blueprint*, which you can also find on Amazon), but below are a few basic tips to get you started.

- **Build Profitable Skills:** These are skills that can increase your earning potential and give you more freedom, like sales, copywriting, coding, etc.

- **Improve Your Negotiation Ability:** Doing so will help you become more assertive, negotiate raises, increase your pay, and generate more sales (if you run a business).

- **Shift From Scarcity to Abundance:** Most people exist in scarcity and view money as a finite resource that will run out and not be easily replenished. You need to shift your mindset to believe that money is abundant and resources are easily generated, as this is *actually* the case (billions and billions of dollars flow in and out of pockets every day). Another way to think about this is to play more offense (be on the attack) rather than only defense (protection and scarcity mode) like most people do. If you don't play enough offense, you won't have much to protect anyway.

- **Build a High-Value Social Circle:** Surround yourself with like-minded guys who are also leveling up.
- **Make Asymmetric Bets:** In this context, a "bet" is when the potential upside far outweighs the potential downside. It could be investing in yourself, taking a shot at a new business, and so on.

As you build yourself up, you can still do everything in this book and women will find you attractive. The better your communication skills, the more leeway women will give you. So get ready to shift into attack mode.

Your "Girl-Getting Machine"

As you start building the above, you'll create what I like to call a "girl-getting machine" for yourself.

Basically, you'll be able to generate a very high number of leads (new women coming into your life) with minimal effort and significantly increase your leverage in the dating market...really to the point where it'll be orders of magnitude above the average guy. When the average guy tells you that he struggles to get dates, you simply won't be able to relate with him because it's so far out of your current reality.

The fly-wheel effect of momentum will be fully in motion, and here's how:

You'll Get More Matches & Dates

The matches will roll in at five to ten times (or more) than what the average guy gets, so you'll have a lot more volume to work with on that front.

At the same time, those matches will lead to dates much more often than before. That's because your dating profile can be good enough to get a match, but not good enough to turn that match into a date. As mentioned earlier, women have significantly more options online, and attractive women will get a match 99% of the time that they swipe right. What this means for you is that you don't just compete to get a match—you compete with the other matches to get a date.

Once you've built a premium brand, you'll win these competitions more often than not and actually flip the script. You'll get so many matches and date opportunities that you'll need to tighten your filter and be more selective with the women you go on dates with. Soon enough, you'll have quite an abundant dating life, and you can narrow those options down to find your most ideal fit.

Again, this is a night and day difference compared to how the average guy finds a girlfriend. He basically takes what he can get and makes dating decisions out of scarcity, and this almost guarantees that he won't meet his ideal mate.

Your In-Person Success Rate Will Improve

As you go on more dates and gain more experience interacting with women, you'll feel more and more comfortable around them. This will lead to better dates and better approaches, which will, in turn, lead to more dates (more first dates, second dates, third dates, and beyond).

One-, two-, and three-date weeks will be fully in your control to create. Compare this to the average guy who maybe lands a date or two every three to four months.

Women Will Take You More Seriously

As your communication skills and comfort level around women increase, women will see you more seriously as a potential mate. You won't make as many mistakes as novice guys that she rules out, and she'll feel like you're one of the guys who "gets it." And so, more women will invite you into their "inner world" and show you sides of themselves that they just wouldn't show to the other guys (even to some of their past boyfriends who, in many cases, just didn't "get it"). They'll respect you more, too, and perceive you as having much higher value—a "catch," if you will.

All This Will Provide Positive Reference Experiences & Compound Your Confidence

At this point, the flywheel effect is indeed in full effect. You now operate in a dating world that most men simply can't even fathom and will never come close to experiencing—abundance, options, and as much control over your dating life as you could want.

You can generate dates from in-person approaches, online dating apps, Instagram, and social events. The women you date want to see you again and again, and they're the first ones to bring up the relationship talk because they're so enamored with you. And now you have enough volume to make one of the biggest decisions of your life.

You Greatly Accelerate Your Path to Meet Your Dream Partner

If you're reading this book, in the back of your mind (aside from just improving with conversation) you likely want to eventually find your dream partner—that amazing woman you can build a healthy relationship with, and maybe even start a family with one day.

Now, as we've covered, most men make this choice out of a place of scarcity and minimal experience. They don't know the red flags to look for, they haven't tapped into their potential as men, and they haven't felt what it's like to have any sort of control over their dating life.

And with all that being the case, it's unlikely that they'll make a great choice. It becomes much easier to "settle" for a less-than-ideal mate because they're not confident that they can attract a similar (or better) mate in the future. That's part of the reason that there are so many unhappy relationships and divorces nowadays. For the man, settling like this sometimes leads to feelings of deep regret; other times, they drown out the sorrow and have a midlife crisis. Either way, it's not exactly the recipe for a happy and fulfilling life.

But it doesn't have to be that way for you. As you go down this path and create the type of abundance most men can only dream of, you greatly accelerate things.

If out of every ten dates there are two or three women who you see long-term potential with, you'll get there a *lot* faster if you're able to score two to three dates a week than if you get two to three dates a year.

And, more importantly, you're in more control and can do things on your terms rather than hoping that things will just magically work out, as most guys do. And I don't know about you, but that seems like a much better place to be in!

Now, let's get on with the rest of Part II. Keep all this in mind as you read through the rest of the book, and start applying these strategies to build your premium brand and create your "girl-getting machine!"

Key Takeaways

- **Online Dating and IG Are Key:** Optimizing these is the easiest way to immediately stand out in the dating marketplace, especially as a busy guy. Do not neglect these.
- **Optimize Your Look:** The more you max out your "genetic potential" in the looks department, the more attention you'll get from women, the more confident you'll feel, and the better you'll perform.
- **Make the "Girl-Getting Machine" Work for You:** When this is going full throttle, you can line up dates, meet more women you're excited about, and fast track your way to meeting your next girlfriend

If you want help building a great dating profile, you'll love **The Top-Tier Dating Profile Kickstart**.

It shows you exactly how to create a high-quality dating profile that can boost your matches by five to ten times overnight.

To get instant access (plus four other exclusive dating bonuses), head over to daveperrotta.com/mastery.

What To Do When You're Scared To Talk To Girls

Luckily for you, there are billions of women on the planet, so it's not difficult to find one to start a conversation with. And yet, so many men have trouble with this due to a combination of fear and insecurity.

They're afraid that women will reject them, and even if they somehow make it through the first part of the conversation, they're afraid that they'll run out of things to say.

This means that they rarely initiate conversations, and as a result, they don't meet nearly as many women as they could.

In the coming sections, you'll learn exactly what to say to keep the conversation flowing. First, though, we have to get you through the beginning.

But before we do that, I want to bring up something that seems to be a common perspective from guys nowadays...

Is Approaching Women Even Worth It?

So why not just get the online dating and Instagram dialed in and forget about approaching girls in person? Sure, you *could* do that, and there are plenty of guys who do. But here's my honest take on it.

I like to have as much control as possible with things that are important to me. Specifically, I never want to feel "helpless" or like I'm unable to do something I want. I'd much rather have the freedom to do what needs to be done without needing to hold back.

That's why, for me, approaching girls will never go out of style.

Think about it: Do you want to be in a situation where you see a beautiful girl walking by but you can't do anything about it? Or do you want to feel confident in your ability to go up to her, start a conversation, and get her attracted?

For me, it'll *always* be the latter. Some of the most amazing connections and girlfriends I've had have been from those "spur of the moment" interactions.

The other thing I'll point out? Not every girl is online all the time.

One pattern I've noticed is a lot of high-quality girls might download a dating app, go on a few dates, and then delete the app until the next month when she decides to use it again. And some don't even use the apps at all.

By totally pigeonholing yourself into online dating, you miss out on a whole subset of girls who aren't there frequently (or at all).

Now, if you're like me, and you want to have as much control as possible of your dating life—along with your full pick of dating options—let's examine how to overcome that fear of starting the conversation!

How to Overcome The Fear of Approaching

You're in line at the supermarket. You look over to the next register line and a beautiful girl catches your eye. You admire her hair and her style, and you smile for a moment—she's exactly your type.

"Credit or debit?" the cashier repeats as you snap back to reality and hand her your card. You sign the receipt and grab your bags—but when you look back at the girl, she's gone.

"Damn!" you think to yourself. You missed your shot. But as you walk out the door, you see her walking right in front of you. You clam up for a second, wondering if you should make your move or let her go.

The excuses start flooding your brain: "She probably has a boyfriend" or "She's a little too tall for me anyway" or "She looks like she's in a rush" or "I'd have to catch up to her to say 'hi,' and that feels weird"—any of these sound familiar?

So what do you do?

There are three possible scenarios:

1. You listen to your excuses, do nothing, and let her go.
2. You approach her and it goes well.
3. You approach her and it doesn't work out the way you wanted.

I was in this exact situation the other day.

At first, I succumbed to my excuses—and I felt terrible about it.

But when she stopped on the street corner for a minute, I swallowed my pride and went for it. The result? She gave me a big smile, and a minute or two later, I walked away with her phone number and plans for drinks.

I felt the fear and did it anyway.

So—what was going through my head right then, and what can you do to propel yourself forward when you're in the same situation? How can you start seizing the opportunities instead of letting them slip through your fingers?

It comes down to the five actions outlined below.

1. Focus on Overcoming Your Fear

If you're afraid to approach her, it actually works in your favor.

See, boldly confronting your fear can feel far more rewarding than simply starting a conversation with a random girl. Consider this quote from the late American business magnate Henry Ford:

"One of the greatest discoveries a man makes, one of his great surprises, is to find he can do what he was afraid he couldn't do."

When you focus on confronting and overcoming the fear, you'll not only approach more women but you'll also grow as a man.

You'll realize, "I had all these excuses and this story that I was telling myself. But I approached her anyway. I did what I was afraid I couldn't do." And it'll feel awesome.

2. Shift Your Perspective

Often, the reason you're afraid to approach her is because you feel like it's too risky. She could reject you and damage your ego. Or maybe she'll respond well but then you'll run out of things to talk about.

In the moment, these fears are actually perfectly reasonable. It's easier and more comfortable for you to do nothing than to take action, and the risk of rejection and embarrassment doesn't feel worth it.

When you're afraid to approach her, your risk spectrum looks like this:

Risk of approaching her: You'll have an awkward interaction, get rejected, and feel terrible—a big risk.

Risk of doing nothing: No risk whatsoever—you'll save your ego, stay in your comfort zone, and move on like nothing happened.

But you need to shift your perspective so that it's actually riskier *not* to approach her.

You need to adjust your understanding of the risks like this:

Risk of approaching her: Potential awkward interaction with a girl you'll probably never see again. One or two minutes of discomfort—a small risk.

Risk of doing nothing: You miss out on a potential amazing connection and incredible intimacy with a woman you're attracted to—a big risk.

Risk of building the habit of not approaching: You signal to your subconscious that it's okay not to approach women you're interested in. In doing so, you miss out on other great girls in the future—another big risk.

With this perspective, it's riskier for you to do nothing than to approach her.

Use this reversal of risk to propel you forward and get the women you want. Make a conscious effort to view approaching women from this perspective. Here's another quote to ponder from ancient historian Herodotus, which basically says it all:

"It is better by noble boldness to run the risk of being subject to half the evils we anticipate than to remain in cowardly listlessness for fear of what might happen."

3. Stop Waiting for the Right Moment

Don't waste time waiting for precisely the right time, because you won't find it—you'll always have an excuse in your head as to why it's the wrong moment.

Instead of waiting, make a habit of taking a step in the direction of the girl you want to talk to. Don't comb your brain for the perfect thing to say, and don't pause.

Just start walking toward her.

She could be talking to her friend, on the phone, eating lunch at an outdoor patio—it doesn't matter. If you don't talk to her now, you probably won't get another chance. And if you wait too long, you'll build up the fear in your head and psyche yourself out.

As I always say, if you point out a girl and tell me to approach her right now, I can do it no problem. But if you point a girl out and tell me to approach her in five minutes from now? Well, that's a whole different ball game. It's going to be a *lot* tougher because I'll be building it up in my head for those five minutes rather than if I'd just taken immediate action.

So take the first step—the action will help you conquer the fear.

Acknowledge your excuses and then let them go.

4. Tap Into Your Manhood

Why do you want to approach her? Well, because on some level, she gives you the feels—you find her attractive and intriguing.

But often, you leave your attraction on the backburner and instead focus on the fear of approaching.

All these thoughts start going through your head: "Does she like me?" "Should I try to kiss her?" "What should I talk about?" "What if she thinks I'm boring?"

Instead, you need to keep your attraction and appreciation for her beauty at the forefront of your mind. This will help you cultivate a nervous excitement instead of a nervous fear—an excitement to meet and learn more about her.

How do you do that? Start by asking yourself: What do you like about her?

Do her eyes draw you in and captivate you? Is her smile contagious? Is her rhythm attractive? Does she make you laugh? Bring these thoughts to the front of your mind.

As you appreciate her inner and outer beauty, you'll be more in tune with your natural male instincts. For me, it always brings a smile to my face and leads me to make strong eye contact. It also allows me to be more free-flowing and in the moment.

When you approach her with this excitement, she'll often mirror you. Even if she isn't into you at first, she'll begin to find you intriguing and feel the same type of excitement.

So tap into your manhood and focus on what you find attractive about her—this will make it easier to approach her, and she'll usually respond positively.

5. Know Your Opener

This is the simplest tip of all, but it may work the best.

Guys freeze up when they see a cute girl because they don't know what to say, but when you have a few openers in mind, you solve that problem. You just need to go up and deliver the words.

Throughout both books in this bundle, you have a bevy of conversation starters that you can use for just about any situation you find yourself in with a woman.

Here's what I recommend:

- Have a conversation starter that you can use in just about any situation (like one of the more direct openers). If all else fails and you can't think of anything, just use that.

- Add the openers throughout the book to a notes app on your phone, organized by different environments, and you can take a look at them whenever you're *in* those environments. Grocery store? Great, you can use the avocado line, for example.

I'll level with you, though: The fear of approaching a new girl will always be there. You can never completely eliminate it. But that's okay—because you don't need to.

A little fear is what makes the process fun and rewarding.

So keep these five actions in mind to help you conquer fear when you feel like it's overwhelming you, and you'll level up on your approaching prowess and get the conversation started with ease.

Key Takeaways (short and sweet and to the point this time):

1. Focus on overcoming your fears.
2. Shift your perspective.
3. Stop waiting for the right moment.
4. Tap into your manhood.
5. Know your opener.

Part 3: Initiate The Conversation

5 Ways to Start a Conversation With Any Girl

You now have a gameplan to conquer your fear of approaching women and become the high-value man that women yearn for. But once you approach them, what do you say? How do you start the conversation? We briefly covered some ideas in the last chapter when we looked at tip #5 ("Know Your Opener"), but it can often be a bit more complicated than pulling out the at-the-ready avocado line in the grocery store.

But before we get into that, let's go over a quick recap from Book 1 of where to meet attractive women:

- Gym and fitness classes
- Grocery stores
- Parks
- The mall
- Busy downtown areas
- Boardwalks and the beach
- Coffee shops and lunch spots
- The farmer's market
- Bookstores and libraries
- Upscale bars and lounges
- Dating apps and Instagram

Now, *what you say* to start the conversation depends on a few things, like:

- **The environment.** The way you start a conversation during the day may be a bit different than the way you start the conversation at a nightclub.

- **The woman.** If she's in a rush, you'll have to move the conversation quickly. But if she's standing and watching a street performer or slowly walking, you know that she has some time, and there'll be plenty of things to talk about.
- **Your goals.** Maybe you're not super interested in the girl and you just want to build some social momentum. Or maybe your intuition literally forced you to talk to this girl because she caught your eye so strongly.

Whatever the situation, this chapter will help you start the conversation properly and move things forward with her.

Keep in mind that when you're in a naturally social environment—perhaps a social sport, house party, or get-together with new friends—you can be more casual with the way you start a conversation. That's because things are expected to be a little more loose in these types of situations. We'll go over this in a bit as well.

1. Going Direct

In this kind of scenario, you basically state your interest from the beginning. This is one of my favorite ways to start a conversation because it cuts through the fluff.

When It's Best to Use: Anytime, but ideally in daytime environments.

You can say:

"Hey, I know this is really random, but I saw you walking by and I thought you were cute, so, I had to say hi. I'm Dave."

It's very important to say this one slowly, make eye contact, and shake her hand afterward.

You want to say it like this:

"Hey…I know this is *reaaaallly* random…but I saw you walking by…and I thought you were cute…so I had to say hi'…I'm Dave."

By delivering it slowly, you'll come across as more confident and she'll hang on to your words. By shaking her hand, you'll initiate physical touch from the beginning, which will make her more comfortable with you.

Going direct is powerful because it shows confidence, and if she stays in the conversation, it's a sign that she's at least somewhat interested in you.

2. Situational

In this case, you pick out something from the environment and use it to start the conversation.

When It's Best to Use: At a bar or club, or when the two of you are otherwise stationary.

For example, let's say that the two of you are staring at one of those street performers who pose as a statue.

You can say:

"I always confuse these things with real statues. My friends always make fun of me for it." This is a fun, tongue-in-cheek way to initiate the conversation.

If you're in a bar or club, you could even say something simple like, "Your drink looks awesome! What is it?"

The key is to deliver this with a slight smile so she knows that you're being playful. You want it to come across in more of a fun way rather than a serious tone.

The situational conversation starter can be powerful because it already gives you a topic to discuss, and it can also be a great way to make her laugh from the beginning. However, make sure not to stay on the topic for too long, as it can go stale and get boring.

3. The "Where is Starbucks?" Approach

This one's simple yet effective: You're walking down the street, and you stop a girl and ask her where the nearest Starbucks is.

When It's Best to Use: During the day while you're walking in a city that has Starbucks locations (if that city doesn't have any, any other popular café or restaurant will do).

Here's the key to pulling this one off:

First, spot the girl you want to talk to—ideally, she'll be walking toward you on the sidewalk. Once you're within ten feet of her, slowly raise your hand in front of you to get her attention. If done right, she'll see your hand and your eye contact before she gets to you.

Then, plant your feet and stop in front of her. Ask, "Hey, do you know where the nearest Starbucks is?"

Before she can fully respond, cut her off and say, "Actually, I just thought you were cute, and I wanted to meet you. I'm Dave."

It's important to do this *before* she finishes giving you directions—we all know that the social tendency is to give quick directions and then immediately walk away.

This conversation starter is powerful because it allows you to gauge her vibe and attractiveness before you show interest. For example, simply by her response and the way she starts to deliver it, you can tell how open she is to having a conversation with you. If she smiles and lights up a little bit, you know that you have a solid chance to make something happen. If she seems cold and dismissive, it might be better to move on.

Plus, if she's not as attractive as you thought she was from afar, you can just ask the Starbucks question and let her give you the directions before walking away. It's very low risk.

4. The Simple Introduction

You don't try to get too cute here. You just give her a simple, "Hey, how's it going?" or a "Hey, I'm Dave. How's it going?"

When It's Best to Use: At bars and clubs and in other social environments.

It's important to deliver this with confidence, strong eye contact, and a lower tone of voice. Otherwise, you'll come across in a platonic "just friends" sort of way, and you'll often get brushed off.

This approach is powerful because of its simplicity—you don't have to dig for what to say. You know that you have this simple conversation starter in your back pocket.

5. The Opinion Opener

If you want a low-pressure way to break the ice, opinion openers are golden. They allow you to spark interest and engage women in a way that feels natural and entertaining.

There are three keys to a successful opinion opener:

1. **It's Relevant:** It should be a topic that's easy for anyone to have an opinion on. Bonus points if it's relevant to the setting or current social context.
2. **It's Open-Ended:** Avoid yes or no questions—you want to encourage her to elaborate and get a discussion going.
3. **It's Light and Fun:** Keep it light rather than engaging in controversial, heavier topics like politics.

Let's look at a few examples of opinion openers:

- **At a Coffee Shop:** "Hey, I'm in a heated debate with my friend about this and we need a tiebreaker. Which is the better coffee order: iced or hot? What's your verdict?"
- **In a Bookstore:** "Excuse me, I'm trying to buy a gift for my sister and I'm torn between these two books. Which one do you think would make a better gift for someone who loves stories with strong female leads?"
- **At an Art Exhibit:** "I'm curious, if you had to take one piece of art from here home with you, which one would it be and why?"
- **At a Nightlife Venue:** "All right, what's the perfect 'after club' late-night snack: street tacos or pizza?"

Once she gives her opinion, you can have some fun with the response. Usually, the best way is to add in a little tease.

For example:

- "You're a pizza girl? I'm all about the street tacos. This'll never work."
- "If I go with this book and my sister hates it, you're getting all the blame."

You can also dig into her response a little bit and get her to expand on it:

- "So you're more into abstract art then?"
- "Pizza? All right let me guess—you've probably got some Italian roots?"

There you have it—you now have five ways to start a conversation with any woman and in any environment.

To see some older videos of me putting these conversation tactics into action during real conversations, **you can check out this playlist on my YouTube channel:** https://bit.ly/daveperrotta.

You no longer have an excuse not to approach and start conversations with women you desire.

In the next chapter, we'll put this knowledge into action.

Key Takeaways:

- **Direct Openers:** State your interest from the beginning. Best to use anytime, especially in daytime environments.
- **Situational Openers:** Pick something from the environment, using that to start the conversation. Best to use in nighttime interactions or when the two of you are otherwise stationary.
- **The "Where is Starbucks?" Approach:** Ask for directions to Starbucks, then cut her off and go direct. This is best to use while walking through a downtown area.
- **The Simple Introduction:** Simply say, "Hey, I'm Dave. How's it going?" This is best to use in nighttime environments.
- **The Opinion Opener:** Ask a fun opinion. This one is great to use in any environment.

Action Tip: Pick at least one of these conversation starters and use it *this week*.

What to Say After You Start the Conversation

Does this sound familiar?

"Hey—I know this is random, but I saw you walking by and you caught my eye. I had to meet you," you say before introducing yourself.

"Wow, thanks! I'm Jessica," she replies, shaking your outreached hand.

The conversation shifts back to you, but at that precise moment, your mind goes blank. You mutter something bland, like "Yeah, it's good to meet you..." without adding any more value to the conversation.

"Yes, it is! But I have to run, so have a good day!" she says, dashing off—and away from *you*.

And just like that, in a split second, you've missed your opportunity.

Sucks, right?

We've all been in that type of scenario before. We start off well, but then go blank and the conversation stalls.

So how can you prevent this? What should you say and do after you approach her? That's what this chapter is all about.

Before you do anything else, you need to introduce yourself. All you need to say is something simple like, "I'm Dave, by the way." She'll usually respond with her name too, and when she does, you should shake her hand. This helps build an initial level of comfort and makes it seem like the two of you aren't strangers anymore.

But where do you take it from there?

The Easy Assumption

Once you get the intro out of the way, it's ideal to then infuse something flirty and fun. That's where the easy assumptions come into play.

Simply make a fun assumption about where she's from. For example, let's say you're talking to a girl in New York City.

"You seem like you're from here…I'm getting city girl vibes from you."

The point is to have a little fun with it and do it with a smile. Either you guess right and she says, "Oh, wow—how did you know?!" or you guess wrong and she says, "I *am* from here, but what made you think that?"

And just like that, you have grounds for a flirty conversation. You can stay on that topic for half a minute or so and then transition from that. Either she gives you something easy to work with or you use the question below to keep things going.

The First Question

Once you've introduced yourself and made an assumption, you can have a little banter around that. Then you can simply ask, "What are you up to?"

This is a powerful question because it can instantly tell you her logistics. You'll know one of three things:

- If she's in a rush
- If she has a few minutes to talk
- If she has a lot of time

You may get a response like:

- "I'm on my way back to work."
- "I'm just hanging out and doing a little shopping."
- "I'm meeting a friend in a little while."

These responses will present you with three different types of situations—along with several directions in which you can take the conversation.

Let's look at some situations you'll face after approaching a girl for the first time, as well as how you can handle each of them.

Situation #1: She's in a Rush

She stops to talk to you, but she's clearly in a rush. You can usually pick up on this through her vibe or simply by the way she answers your "What are you up to?" question.

So what should you do if you've only got a minute or less to talk to her? A lot of guys think this isn't enough time to do anything, but they're wrong.

If you think she's attractive and you'd like to see her again, you should *still* ask for her number. It doesn't matter that you've just met her—you literally have nothing to lose.

Here's what you should say if she's in a rush:

"I know this is random and we literally just met, but you have a really fun vibe. Would you like to hang out sometime?"

By saying, "I know this is random and we just met," you signal that you have social intelligence (in other words, that you're aware of the randomness of the situation) while also addressing her potential objection of "But we just met!" *before* she can even say it.

If she says, "Yeah, that sounds fun!", you can say, "Okay, awesome!" Then pull out your phone, go to the "add contact" screen, hand it to her, and tell her to input her number.

If she says something along the lines of "no" followed by an excuse (like "I have a boyfriend"), you can say, "No worries—just take it as a compliment then," and exit the conversation.

Situation #2: She Has a Few Minutes to Talk

She lets you know that she's meeting up with a friend in a few minutes, or perhaps she's at the beginning of her lunch break from work. You can tell that she's not in a huge rush, but she *does* have somewhere to be in a little while.

Your goal here should be to make a good first impression and get her number at a high point in the conversation. All you really have to do here is make an assumptive statement—just make a guess about her as mentioned above.

Two other assumptive statements you can make:

1. What she does for a living: "You seem like you do something creative."

2. What type of person she is: "You seem like a fun, adventurous kind of person."

These statements will give you some solid, fun, conversational material. From here, you should be able to keep the conversation going for two or three minutes.

Then, when the conversation seems to be at a high point (the two of you are laughing, realizing that you have something in common, etc.), tell her that you need to go and then ask for her number.

You can say something like, "Listen, it's been great to meet you. I gotta run, but you seem like a lot of fun. Would you like to hang out sometime?"

Once she says "Yes!", pull out your phone and have her put her number in.

Situation #3: She's Got a Lot of Time on Her Hands

After approaching her, you realize that she's not really doing much right now. She's not in a rush and she doesn't have to be anywhere.

Here, you have two options:

1. Take her on an "instant date."
2. Talk to her for a little while and grab her number (similar to Situation #2 above).

We'll get into both of these scenarios in a second, but first let's dive into some more conversational tools you can use to extend the conversation.

Aside from making statements, you can also:

- Ask open-ended questions ("What brings you to this city?"), then listen and relate back with your own experiences.
- Compliment her in genuine and unique ways ("You have a very unique style—I might need to get some fashion tips from you.").
- Playfully tease her ("Oh, you're from LA? You're a Valley girl at heart, aren't you?").

These tips will help you extend the conversation and connect with her.

We're going to go over all these conversational tactics throughout the rest of the book—this is just a brief introduction to them.

Okay, now let's get back to those two options mentioned previously.

How to Take Her on an "Instant Date"

With this option, you can say, "I'm not in a big rush right now and you seem like fun. I know a great coffee place down the street. What do you say we check it out?"

The benefit of an "instant date" like this is that it can create a deeper connection and more familiarity with the girl. But the danger is that it can also lead to you getting friend-zoned.

For it to work well, you need to maintain the flirtatious, man-to-woman type of vibe throughout the interaction. This can sometimes be difficult in a daytime setting if you don't have a lot of experience.

As for the second scenario—talking to her for a little while and grabbing her number—you basically just do the same thing as you would if she had a few minutes to talk. Maybe you stay in for a few extra minutes and use the three conversation tips from this section. Then you get her number at a high point in the interaction and leave.

You now have a solid structure to handle most of the situations when you'll be approaching a girl. Internalize this structure and you won't have to worry about "running out of things to say" after you approach her.

You'll be able to make the conversation interesting and truly connect with her. In doing so, you'll give yourself the best chance to get her number and see her again.

Key Takeaways:

- **Use Easy Assumptions:** These will help you move the conversation in a flirty direction and create fun banter.
- **Figure Out Her Logistics:** Ask "What are you up to?" early in the conversation—this tells you if she's in a hurry or has a bit of time to talk.
- **If She's in a Rush:** Keep it short and be respectful of her time. Go for her number within the first minute or two.
- **If She Has Time to Talk:** You can extend the conversation a few minutes longer, or potentially invite her for an "instant date."

Action Tip: Approach a girl sometime within the next 24 hours. Use one of the conversation starters from the last section and follow it up by introducing yourself, making assumptions, and asking what she's up to.

Part 4: Connect

Get Her Talking

You now have a basic framework for building a conversation with women, but you still need to know the nitty-gritty behind developing longer conversations. That way, you'll be properly equipped to go on dates and build a fun, flirty, deeper connection.

And to do that, you need to get her talking, because the more she talks about herself, the more she'll feel connected to you.

In this section, you'll learn how to do exactly that: move past the small talk and get her talking about herself.

Let's get started.

Get Past the Small Talk and Connect With Her

Small talk—the barren wasteland of conversation that seems so hard to move beyond. When you're in small talk mode with a woman you're interested in, you're basically treading water.

Even if you start the conversation well, you still need to get to know her and move beyond the basic stuff, like where she's from and what she thinks of the weather. You need to stir up some emotions.

But this can seem like a daunting task, especially when your conversational counterpart is a beautiful woman. Your mind either draws a blank or starts running a million miles per minute.

"What do I say? What if she rejects me? What if she gets bored?"

That's when you fall into "interview mode," in which you ask basic questions that require a one- or two-word answer. The result? The conversation stalls out, and then you beat yourself up over it.

Here's what happens when you constantly engage in small talk:

- She'll flake and you'll be ghosted more often.
- She won't remember you.
- She won't feel that "spark."
- And, even worse, she'll feel like you don't understand her.

If this sounds familiar to you, don't sweat it. It happens to every guy at one point or another. But there's an easy way to make the conversation flow—and it doesn't require you to employ a bunch of intricate conversation tricks. Actually, you don't even have to talk all that much.

In fact, if you're doing it right, the girl will be talking more than *you*.

So, how can you beat small talk, make the conversation flow, **and build a connection? It comes down to a combination of the following:**

- Asking the right questions
- Listening and relating
- Avoiding common conversation mistakes

We'll cover each one of these in this chapter.

Asking the Right Questions

A few simple, pointed questions can draw her interest, open the conversation, and help you plow past the small talk.

Think about it: When you're in "interview mode," she doesn't even have to think. She can basically respond on autopilot because she's had that same type of conversation hundreds of times with other (boring) guys.

But when you ask the *right* questions, you cause a pattern interrupt. Suddenly, she has to think—she has to ponder her motivations and actually feel things. Beyond that, you also allow her to talk about herself, her passions, and her motivations. This instantly breaks you out of small talk mode.

I'll give you some powerful (but simple) questions to point you in the right direction, but more importantly, you'll learn how to structure your questions so that you can further the conversation instead of leading it to a dead end of awkward silence.

If you do this right, you'll be able to transform women from being cold and closed off to warm and open.

Sidenote: These questions, along with the question structure, are relevant to any conversation, whether you're chatting with the hottie at the bar, at a networking event, or in any kind of random situation you find yourself in.

Why Questions Are Important

This seems counterintuitive, but when you prompt people to tell you about themselves, they actually perceive you as more interesting…even if they barely know anything about you.

Scientists have found that talking about ourselves activates the same pleasure centers of the brain that are associated with food and money. [1]

And the best way to prompt people to do so is to ask them the right questions—ones that allow the other person to open up to you and talk about the stuff they really care about.

By asking the right questions and taking the time to listen to the person's responses, you'll get paid back tenfold. They'll undoubtedly reciprocate and show a lot of interest in *your* life.

How to Structure Your Questions

There are two main types of questions we'll deal with here, so let's outline them below.

Short-Answer Questions: Ask too many of these types of questions in a row and you'll find yourself deep in "interview mode"—you'll be on a conversational path that leads to nowhere. **These are the kinds of questions that only require a one-word response, like:**

- "Where did you go to school?"
- "What do you do?"
- "Where are you from?"

Now, it's okay to ask these types of questions, especially at the beginning of the conversation. In fact, it's almost necessary. But unless you follow up with open-ended questions, the conversation will fall flat.

Open-Ended Questions: These questions require a deeper, extended response—more than a one word "yes" or "no" answer. These are your money questions. If you can master these, you'll be able to open up almost any conversation. **Here's how you can mix these in with short-answer questions:**

You: "What do you do?" **(short-answer question)**

Her: "I'm a lawyer."

You: "Cool, cool. How did you get into that?" **(open-ended question)**

Her: "Well, my dad was a lawyer, and ever since I was a kid, I've been in love with the idea of defending people and going to bat for them."

You: "Oh wow, that's awesome. What do you like about it?" **(open-ended question)**

Her: "Well, I really like helping people and…"

The key with open-ended questions is that you need to dig a little deeper. For example, as illustrated above, instead of asking "Do you like it?", ask her instead *what* she likes about it.

And remember—you need to balance short-answer questions with open-ended questions.

Below are some powerful open-ended questions to ask:

- What do you like about your job?
- What was it like growing up in [where she grew up]?
- If you could wake up anywhere in the world tomorrow, where would it be?
- What's your dream job?
- Why are you doing [this] instead of [that]?

Listening & Relating

Questions are important, but you shouldn't just rattle question after question at her—even if they're effective, open-ended questions.

This is a big mistake that guys make. Instead of actively listening to a woman, they nod along with a blank stare or wait for her to stop talking so that they can say what they want. When you don't actively listen, it makes women feel like you don't understand them. In fact, they feel like you don't even really care.

So what should you do instead?

When she tells you about herself, actively listen to her and relate back to her responses. Provide some sort of feedback, even if it's as simple as repeating back what she said.

For example, let's say that she tells you about how she loved studying abroad in Spain. You could respond with, "That's awesome that you lived in Spain! I've been learning Spanish, and it's definitely on my list of places to go."

She might say, "That's great! I absolutely recommend it."

To which you could respond, "Great! So what made you want to live there?"

This shows that you listen and you "get it," and it also allows her to reveal her motivations to you, providing a strong, emotional topic. Plus, it shows that you're interested in her as well. This eases the social pressure and makes her feel like you're on her side.

Here's another example:

You: "What do you do?"

Her: "I'm an architect."

You: "Ah, that's awesome. One of my favorite parts of walking through NYC is looking at all the beautiful architecture. It's crazy how the city is filled with so many beautiful buildings. You must get some inspiration from them, right?"

Her: "Yeah! The buildings here are incredible."

You: "For sure. So tell me, what made you want to get into architecture?"

Her: "Well, I've always loved creating things. Ever since I was a kid, I dreamed of designing a building that would be part of the NYC skyline."

You: "Oh yeah? It sounds like you're doing something you're really passionate about! So what kind of building do you love to design the most?"

Avoiding Common Conversation Mistakes

The more you get past the small talk, the more risks you'll take in conversations—and the more potential mistakes you will be exposed to.

That's why I'm going to highlight a few "mistakes" for you to be aware of. These mistakes will make you come across as rude or make the girl feel as though you don't "get" her.

These mistakes are all based on a psychological concept known as "the other."

Do you ever feel like there are the people who "get you" and then there's everybody else? People who just understand you and your lifestyle, and then the people who can't even begin to relate to you? That's what I mean by "the other."

See, we have a tendency to view everything in the world (including other human beings) as being either the "same" as ourselves or "other" (i.e., "with us" or "against us").

And rightfully so. This "same vs. other" concept protects us from potential threats and helps us stick with the people who understand us best and are most likely to support us.

But when it comes to seducing and connecting with women, it's where many guys destroy their chances. That's because many guys are great at positioning themselves as "the other" and not very good at showing how they're "the same." But in order to emotionally connect with women, you need for them to see you as the "same" as them.

So the goal of highlighting these mistakes is to help you stop doing things that make women view you as "the other" so that you can make connections with them.

Mistake #1: Stating Contentious Opinions

Let's say that you love to meditate. You're on a date with a girl and she says, "You know what I can't stand? People who meditate. They just sit there doing nothing and claim that it clears their mind. What a waste of time."

How would you feel? Probably much less connected to her, right?

This is exactly what you want to avoid doing to her. There's really no reason for stating contentious opinions early on—it only puts you at risk of ruining the connection.

Solution #1: Be Non-Judgmental & Focus on Commonalities

When you're trying to connect with a girl, it's best to avoid arguments and contention. These will put you in the "other" category faster than anything else.

If you hate 9-to-5 jobs and cubicles but she works a desk job that she enjoys, it's probably not a great idea to go on about how much you despise conventional jobs (I've made this mistake many times).

Instead, focus on things that you can easily relate to each other on, like interests and hobbies. For example, maybe you both like to travel and read, or have a favorite Netflix show in common.

Sidenote: It's okay to disagree with girls without being contentious. Just avoid making it a big deal or a major part of the conversation.

Some guys may say, "No, I'd rather state a contentious opinion because if she disagrees, there's no point to continue seeing her."

I get it—but there are better ways to do it. You can gradually figure out her values and interests as you go further into the conversation without making it seem like you're judging her.

If she's got a viewpoint you want to know more about, you can dig into it a bit, figure out what gave her that perspective, and how closely held it is. If she has an opposing view to you on something you see as important but you can tell it's not strongly held, there may be some wiggle room there.

Mistake #2: Getting Married to a Conversation Topic

You know that feeling when you're done talking about something but your conversation counterpart keeps bringing it back up? Every conversation topic has a lifespan, and if you try to milk the topic past that point, you'll annoy people (and turn women off).

You may be tempted to do this because you're naturally more comfortable with certain conversation topics. For example, if you enjoy working out, you're likely comfortable talking about lifting weights. But you can't allow yourself to keep falling back to this topic—you must keep the conversation flowing. And you'll accomplish this with the next solution below.

Solution #2: Weave in Multiple Topics

A rich conversation weaves through a variety of topics.

It's okay to change the subject, even if you haven't said everything you feel like you need to say about something. But when you keep reverting back to a conversation topic, it signals to women that you have low social intelligence—and also that you're not a very well-rounded man.

If you're tempted to keep coming back to a "dead" topic, stop yourself and ask a solid question to push the conversation forward (e.g., "What are you passionate about?").

It's also important to keep the conversation focused on more emotional topics, which can include:

- Her dreams
- Her experiences
- Things she loves to do
- What she's passionate about
- What her motivations are

(We'll delve further into these emotional conversation topics in the next chapter.)

There *are* times when you can return to a topic, but it's best not to do it frequently. And if you do go back to it, put a little bit of a different spin on it so that it can morph into a new topic. Basically, you use that old topic as a springboard.

For example, if you move onto a new topic that eventually starts dying out, you can say something like, "Oh, that reminds me. So I know that you went to Italy...but where else would you love to travel to?"

Mistake #3: Talking Too Much About Yourself

A friend told me that she went on a Tinder date the other day with a doctor. He was handsome, successful, and wealthy—everything a woman wants, right? But within an hour, she had her friend call her and give the "sick grandma excuse" so that she could escape this terrible date.

(The "sick grandma excuse," by the way, is when a girl has her friend call her 30 minutes to an hour into a date. If she's having fun, the girl will hang up and continue on with the date. If she's not, she'll say, "My mom just called—my grandma is sick and I have to go see her." There are variations of this—someone was in an accident or a cousin was just rushed to the hospital—and it's a fairly common escape route for women to easily remove themselves from a date gone wrong.)

So what went wrong with my friend and her doctor date?

Well, the guy ranted and raved about himself, his success, and his "importance." She felt like she couldn't be herself around him and as though he was constantly judging her.

He positioned himself as "the other" right from the beginning—and it killed any attraction and hope for a connection.

Solution #3: Focus the Conversation on Her

You don't have to say that much about yourself, especially in your first conversation. In fact, you can tell her very little while having her open up and tell you almost everything about herself.

Remember—talking about ourselves activates the same pleasure centers of the brain that are associated with food and money. The more she talks about herself, the more connected she'll feel to you.

You can give her bits and pieces here and there about yourself through listening and relating, but you don't need to give her your whole life story. Just let things flow.

Key Takeaways:

- **Get Past the Small Talk:** Ask the right questions to dive deeper, get to know her, and move beyond the platonic level of conversation.
- **Mix Up Your Questions:** Use a mix of short-answer and open-ended questions, then listen and relate back to keep the conversation flowing.
- **Avoid Common Conversation Pitfalls:** Stating contentious opinions, getting married to a conversation topic, and talking too much about yourself will make it harder to connect with her.
- **Correct the Mistakes:** Don't pass judgments, weave in multiple topics, and turn the conversation back over to her rather than talking too much.

Action Tip #1: Write down five open-ended questions, focusing them on emotional topics like we covered above. For example, "What are you most passionate about?"

Action Tip #2: Write down the conversation mistake from the list above that you feel you're most guilty of. This will help you be more aware of it and avoid it in the future.

Reference:

1. Tamir, Diana I., and Jason P. Mitchell. "Disclosing information about the self is intrinsically rewarding." *Proceedings of the National Academy of Sciences* 109.21 (2012): 8038-8043.

5 Go-To Conversation Topics for Connecting

Remember—the more she talks about herself, the more connected she'll feel to you. And in order to truly get her to talk about herself, you need to infuse emotional topics into the conversation.

Sure, it's nice to talk about the new club downtown or the weather, but those are conversations she can have with anyone. You want to move to topics that aren't universally relatable for everyone. That's how real connections are formed, and that's what this chapter is all about.

(Sidenote: It's best to weave these topics into conversation rather than formulaically cycling through them. Allow the conversation to flow and evolve. Also, try to relate back to her responses with something relevant from your own life. This shows her that you "get her," that you're interested, and that you're paying attention.)

With this in mind, let's look at five go-to conversation topics that'll make it easy to talk and connect with women.

1. Her Experiences

Perhaps you've both gone scuba diving or traveled to Vietnam. Or maybe she quit her job and moved to a beach town to become a whale shark tour guide.

We've all had memorable experiences—whether good, bad, uplifting, or scary. And experiences are tied to emotions, so that's why they're such a great topic.

They can lead to amazing stories and tons of feelings, as well as unique ways to relate to each other.

Let's consider some questions that can get you to this topic:

- "What made you want to come to this city?"
- "What was your last big adventure?"
- "Where's your favorite place you've traveled to?"

Once you get her talking about these kinds of things, you can dive deeper and ask questions like:

- "How did it feel when you did that?"
- "What was it like to do that?"
- "Would you change anything about your experience with that?"

When you ask these types of questions, you'll tap into the emotions she felt when she had those experiences.

2. Her Dreams

What does she really want to do with her life? What are her biggest aspirations?

Everybody thinks about their dreams, but not everybody gets to talk about them. That's because most people never think to ask them—we're generally all caught up in our own aspirations.

But given the opportunity, most people would love to talk about their dreams and goals, which is why it brings up all sorts of pleasant and hopeful emotions.

Below are some questions that can get you to this topic:

- "What's something you've always wanted to do?"
- "What's something you want to achieve this year?"
- "What was your biggest dream when you were a kid?"

Once you get her talking about these kinds of things, you can dive deeper and ask questions like:

- "How would it feel to do that?"
- "How would your life change if you accomplish that?"
- "What's stopped you from going for it?"

3. What She Loves to Do

What do you love to do? Think about the answer to that for a minute.

No, really. Do it right now.

Did you think about it? Okay, good.

How did it feel? You probably pictured yourself doing those things that came to mind, and you probably feel similar emotions when you actually do them, right?

For me, I love performing on stage. Every time I think about it, I picture my past performances with huge crowds cheering for me, and I was killing it. It brings up a feeling of excitement.

When women talk about the things they love to do, the same thing happens. They feel those great emotions, and they associate those great emotions with being around you.

Let's look at some questions that can get you to this topic:

- "What do you absolutely love to do?"
- "What kind of activities set you on fire and get you excited?"
- "What kinds of things make you laugh the hardest?"

Once you get her talking about these kinds of things, you can dive deeper and ask questions like:

- "What do you love about that?"
- "How do you feel when you do that?

4. Her Passions

What passions drive her? Maybe she loves traveling, or perhaps she's extremely passionate about volunteering.

Passions are another highly emotional topic—people love talking about them. What's more, a woman's passions can tell you a lot about her, as well as give you a glimpse into whether you're a good fit for each other.

You may find that you have similar passions, which will make it very easy to relate and connect with her.

Here's a question that can get you to this topic: "What are you most passionate about?"

Once you get her talking about this, you can dive deeper and ask questions like:

- "What makes you passionate about that?"
- "How do you feel when you're following that passion?"

5. Her Motivations

Why does she want the things she wants? What are her true motivations? Most men never dig this deep, and it's a big mistake.

They ask questions like, "What do you do?" and she responds with something like, "Oh, I'm a lawyer." He follows up with, "Cool! Do you like it?", to which she responds, "It's okay, and what about you?"

That's the foundation of a boring, polite, platonic conversation—and that's exactly what you don't want.

Instead, try to figure out exactly *why* she wants the things she wants. When you do this from a place of curiosity, it shows that you're interested and not afraid to explore her motivations further. It's quite the pattern interrupt, but that's a good thing.

Below are some questions that can get you to this topic:

- "What made you want to get into that?" (if she's discussing her career or college major)
- "What made you do that?" (if she's discussing a story or a choice she's made)

Once you get her talking about these kinds of things, you can dive deeper and ask questions like:

- "Now that you're doing that, how do you feel about it?"

- "Why did you want to accomplish that?"

The more you explore these kinds of emotional topics, the easier you'll connect with women. You'll stop having those dreaded, polite, "just friends" conversations.

What's more, you'll start sparking attraction with your words and find that a *lot* more women are suddenly into you.

So use these with caution and break them out when you genuinely want to connect with women.

Key Takeaways (bring up these topics to connect):

- **Her Experiences:** This can lead to fun stories and can be an easy way to find commonalities.
- **Her Dreams and What She Loves to Do:** These topics bring up positive emotions, and she'll associate those emotions with you.
- **Her Passions:** These tell you a lot about her and give you a glimpse into whether or not you might be a good fit.
- **Her Motivations:** Asking her above these shows that you're interested, can listen well, and aren't afraid to dive a little deeper.

Action Tip: Choose at least one of these conversation topics and use them in your next conversation with a woman.

Part 5: Captivate

Talking About Yourself in an Attractive Way

She says to you from across the dinner table, "So you know all this stuff about me...I want to know more about *you*!"

"Well, what do you want to know?" you ask her with a sly smile.

"I don't know. What do you do? What's your story?"

So—what are you going to say? How are you going to talk about yourself?

While it's best to get her talking about herself, as well as create a fun, flirty conversation, at some point she'll want to know about you. Whether she asks you for your story or you relate things about your life throughout the conversation, you need to know how to talk about yourself in an attractive way.

But most men do this all wrong. How? In a few ways, as we'll see below.

They Focus on Facts & Stats Over Emotions

Too many men say things like, "Well, I've been to five countries, I have this awesome car, I run a successful business, I'm a doctor..." and so on. And all these things sound nice—impressive, even. But there's one big problem.

Women don't connect with facts and stats. They connect with emotions. And the way to communicate emotionally is to tell better stories and communicate good qualities.

However, there's another problem.

Most Men Are Terrible Storytellers

They infuse their stories with "humble brags" and don't talk about the emotions involved. Instead, they just convey the facts and talk about what happened. What's worse, they don't involve the other person in the story at all. They talk *at* the woman the whole time instead of talking *with* her.

But even when men *do* tell good stories, there's still another problem.

Most Men Don't Convey the Right Qualities About Themselves

See, one of the keys to talking about yourself is to portray attractive qualities. If you don't know the right qualities to convey and how to convey them, you risk killing the connection and making dumb mistakes.

Speaking of mistakes, there's another big one that men make when talking about themselves.

They Give Away Too Much Too Quickly

You don't need to be a completely open book, especially when you first meet somebody.

We've all met that person who seems to give it all up right away. They go into their life story without even being prompted. It's a little off-putting, right?

It's better to hold a little back and be intriguing.

Now, you may be thinking, "Wow, I'm always making a lot of these mistakes!"

That's okay, though. That's why you have this book—to learn how to avoid the common mistakes and communicate more effectively (and attractively). And that's what you're going to learn throughout this chapter.

When you talk about yourself in an attractive way, you can literally "flip" the attraction switch in a woman's mind. If she wasn't into you before, you can open her up to the idea of being with you. And if she was *already* interested in you, you can keep building that interest to the point where she's open to taking the next step (perhaps leaving the bar and going home with you).

So how do you talk about yourself in an attractive way?

There are a few elements to this:

1. Understand the purpose of talking about yourself.
2. Highlight attractive qualities about yourself.
3. Bait her.
4. Follow the proper etiquette.

We'll go into detail for each of these four elements so that you can start talking about yourself attractively.

Step #1: Understand the Purpose of Talking About Yourself

This step is actually quite simple: It's to quickly excite and intrigue her, and then turn the conversation back over to her.

You don't need to tell your life story, convince her why you're the perfect man for her, or list out all your impressive accolades. Just excite her, intrigue her, and get her talking about herself again.

Step #2: Highlight Attractive Qualities About Yourself

How do you excite and intrigue her? It starts by emphasizing the qualities about yourself that are appealing.

Most men *think* that women are attracted to a solid job, lots of money, and good looks. And while these things are all great to have, they aren't at the root of attraction. In other words, they aren't enough.

Just ask the guy who worked his whole life to make a lot of money, assuming that women would love him for it, only to realize later that having a lot of money doesn't do the trick.

When you try to convey these qualities in conversation, you just seem like you're trying to impress the girl. But what qualities are women *actually* attracted to? **There are four main qualities you should keep in mind:**

1. Dominance
2. Sociability
3. Altruism
4. Problem Solving

Let's start with dominance.

Think about how a stereotypical "nice guy" interacts with women. He plays it safe, waits for overwhelming signs of attraction before making a move, and doesn't have much success.

But for women, being with this kind of man is a chore.

Think of how a dominant man acts. Women are an abundant resource for him, so he doesn't put them on a pedestal. He knows what he wants in life and goes for it unapologetically. What's more, women don't have to worry about as much when they're with a dominant man—they can relax, knowing that he'll lead and make them feel positive emotions.

Dominance, then, is an indicator that a guy is successful with women and has control of his life, which makes this trait very attractive to women.

So how can you convey dominance in conversation? The following are some examples:

- A time when you achieved something you once thought was impossible
- How you took charge of a situation even though you were unsure of the outcome
- A time when you successfully led a group of people

Here's a quick example of something a dominant guy might say:

"There was this one camping trip where we were totally lost: maps did nothing, phones had no signal, and it was getting dark. Everyone started freaking out, but I remembered this old trick my grandpa taught me of using the stars to find our way. I wasn't sure it would work, but I managed to lead us back to our site. That night, we had the best campfire stories, all thanks to a bit of skygazing and some levelheadedness."

Now, let's move onto sociability.

A woman wants to feel like she can bring you around her friends without having to worry that you might creep them out or do something cringey.

What's more, sociability signals that you're a cool, confident guy who can talk to *anybody*. The sociable guy communicates with people with ease, has a big social circle, and is well-connected. This signals that he's successful with women and has abundance in his life (with women, friends, and money).

So how can you convey sociability in conversation? Let's look at some examples of things that you might bring up:

- A time when you hung out with a group of friends and had fun
- A time when you connected with someone you looked up to
- A time when you introduced two groups of friends to each other

Here's an example of something a sociable guy might say:

"Last summer, I organized this beach volleyball tournament for charity. Friends, colleagues, and even my old college buddies came down. What started as a simple game turned into this huge event. It wasn't just about the sport—it was about bringing people together for a good cause. And the best part? Watching groups who'd never met before high fiving, planning rematches, and talking about next year's game before the day was even over."

Now let's dive into the concept of altruism.

A study by *Evolutionary Psychology* found that, at least for serious relationships, women value altruism over good looks. In other words, they're more likely to choose an average-looking altruistic man than an attractive but non-altruistic one. [1]

Altruistic behaviors are those intended to help other people. When you're altruistic, you're unselfishly concerned about the rights, feelings, and welfare of other people. Some behaviors you'd associate with altruism are feeling empathy and acting in ways that benefit other people.

Again, let's look at this through a "nice guy" lens. The typical "nice guy" is a little bitter toward women. Most of his actions are meant to get something from other people (especially women) without much of a care for how those other people feel, and so he's not very altruistic.

Now let's compare this with the altruistic man. This guy doesn't do anything with an ulterior motive—instead, he does altruistic and selfless things as an end in themselves.

Essentially, altruism indicates that a man is genuine, caring, and not looking to "get" something from everybody he interacts with.

So how can you convey altruism in conversation? **The following are some examples that you could talk about:**

- A time when you helped somebody less fortunate
- A time when you did some volunteer work
- A time when you helped a friend accomplish something

Here's a quick example of something that an altruistic guy might say:

"Living in Medellin, Colombia was a ton of fun. We had awesome parties and met tons of cool people. But one of the most memorable parts was taking a trip up to the poorest section of the city and handing out shoes to the little kids. Have you ever done volunteer work, by the way? This was my first time. Anyway, these kids either had no shoes or extremely beaten-up shoes. So seeing the looks on their faces when we handed them some brand-new kicks was amazing. The whole experience really put everything into perspective for me."

And finally, let's end with problem solving.

Women *love* men who can solve problems—it's much easier for them to date a man who can get things done and figure out solutions than one who's indecisive, uncertain, and wishy-washy.

On a small scale, it makes things easier for a woman when dating. She knows that a problem-solving man can take charge and plan the dates, direct the conversation forward in the right way, and figure out any logistical hiccups that may come up.

On a big-picture scale, she feels confident that you can solve whatever life throws at the both of you. Finances, career changes, children, moving, and so on—these are all situations that can bring a variety of both good and bad. The average man may have trouble solving these, or do so in suboptimal ways that lead to a more tumultuous life for her. This is also why indecision is such an unattractive trait for men to have.

So if you're a problem solver and can get things done (most men can't), she'll highly value that and want to spend more time with you.

So how do you show off your problem-solving prowess?

Well first, you've actually got to be a good problem solver. You can't fake it.

To achieve this, you must work on:

- Decisiveness
- Self-awareness
- Clarity of thinking
- Problem-solving experience (i.e., don't shy away from problems—tackle them head on. The more you do this, the better you'll get at it)

As you develop this skill, **here's how you can showcase it in interactions and conversations with women:**

- Actually solve logistical problems as they come up on dates and interactions (where to go next, making the plan, passing her tests, working through obstacles that come up, etc.)

- In conversation, bring up times when you solved difficult problems in a satisfying way.

On the flip side, don't try to solve her problems *unless* she asks you to. If she talks about her emotions or an issue at work, don't flip right into problem-solving mode. Instead, hear her out, let her vent, and show her that you understand. At that moment, that's all that you need to do.

However, if she asks you for help with solving a problem, you can step up and solve it, which will get her super attracted to you.

For example, a girl I was dating once had an issue with her upstairs neighbors. They were an opera-singing couple who on a daily basis would frequently belt out these operatic songs at the highest possible volume. It was quite annoying and distracting, as the walls were very thin. For months, this drove my girlfriend crazy until she couldn't take it anymore.

One day she asked me, "Dave, can you help me figure this out?" And trust me—by this point, I'd been hanging at her house for a long enough period of time to be very annoyed by these singers, too.

I agreed to help out. I walked upstairs, knocked on the door, and greeted the male opera singer. I explained the situation, worked through it with him, and found a solution: The couple agreed to only sing for an hour a day at a certain time when my girlfriend and I weren't typically home.

My girlfriend was ecstatic with the solution, and even more enamored with me than she was before. Her respect and attraction for me immediately rose even higher. She'd mention for weeks after that how impressed and relieved she was that I was able to solve the problem—and also how hot it was for her.

To sum all that up: Be a man who can get things done.

So then—dominance, sociability, altruism, and problem solving. If you can convey these qualities, you can come off as very attractive to women.

Aside from these four main qualities, there are some secondary qualities you should highlight as well:

- **Adventurousness:** Women love spontaneous men. They want the kind of guy who's going to make them feel alive, challenge them, and excite them, not the kind of guy they can easily predict.
- **Appreciation of Beauty:** Men who appreciate beauty usually genuinely love women. What's more, they also tend to enjoy good intimacy.
- **Sense of Humor:** Women like a man who can make them laugh and make light of situations compared to a man who takes himself too seriously.

Step #3: Bait Her

When it comes to talking about yourself, it's always more powerful for it to happen when she asks you about something rather than when you straight up tell her on your own. We all know those people who drone on about themselves without prompting, and you don't want to be that guy.

It's far better if she has to dig a little bit to discover more about you, and that's where baiting comes into play.

Baiting causes women to put effort into finding out who you are. It makes you seem a *lot* more interesting and even adds a bit of mystery.

We're going to cover three specific forms of baiting, and you'll want to infuse all of them into your conversations.

Baiting Technique 1: Make an Intriguing Statement

Let's say that a girl is asking you what you do for a living.

You could just spell it out flatly, as in, "I'm an accountant."

Okay, that's fine—but it doesn't give her much to work with. Plus, it paints you as a bit of a boring, typical guy.

Now let's look at how you can answer this in a more intriguing way. When she asks what you do, you can say, "I handle the numbers for different businesses, and when I'm not doing that, I like to dominate on the pickleball court."

This is descriptive but also short on details—it gives her more room to work with. It also makes you seem more intriguing and fun.

Here's another example, this time when she's asking you what you like to do.

You could say something basic such as, "I like reading books and learning in general." Again, a bit of a boring statement. Now let's add some baiting to it:

"I love learning and improving. I feel like if you're not stretching your comfort zone and feeling a little dumb some of the time, you're not really living."

Now she's thinking, "What does he mean by 'learning?' And how has he stretched his comfort zone?"

She's intrigued. She'll want to dig deeper and learn more about you.

Baiting Technique 2: Reciprocity

In his groundbreaking book *Influence*, author Robert Cialdini discusses the six key influence tactics of psychology and persuasion. One of the most powerful of those tactics is reciprocity.

As humans, we generally aim to return favors and pay people back when they've given us something. In other words, we have a strong urge to reciprocate. Have you ever asked to sample more than a couple of flavors at an ice cream shop? After you've tasted a few, do you feel compelled to buy something, even if you don't really have the strong urge to eat any more ice cream?

That's reciprocity in action, and you can use this tactic to bait her in conversations. How? When you dive deep into a particular topic about her life, she'll feel compelled to ask you about that same topic.

For example, let's say that you've used the question structure from Part 3 of this book, and she's told you about her career, what made her get into it, what she likes about it, and so on. Maybe the two of you have spent a few minutes or more discussing it.

She's going to feel a lot of social pressure to reciprocate and ask what *you* do. At that point, you can use the first baiting technique to keep her intrigued and interested.

Baiting Technique 3: The Open Loop

Ever watched the hit series *Game of Thrones*? They end every episode with a huge, open loop that gets you excited and interested in the next episode or the next season. That open loop stays in the back of your mind all week until the next episode airs. It's powerful stuff.

You can also use these open loops in conversation. For example, let's say that she's talking about travel:

Her: "I traveled abroad to Spain when I was in college. It was a great experience."

You: "Spain is one of my favorite countries! What did you think about the culture?"

Her: "It was amazing! So much different than here. The tapas were incredible and the people were so stylish. What'd you think of Spain? And what other countries have you been to?"

Can you spot the open loop in this example? If you missed it, here it is:

"Spain is **one of my favorite countries**! What did you think about the culture?

By telling her that Spain is *one of* your favorite countries, you indirectly signal that you've been to others (and that you have the quality of adventurousness), but then you continue on with an open-ended question.

You've created an open loop in her mind, because she'll be curious about what other countries you've been to. And by following it up with an open-ended question about her, you do it in a socially savvy way.

If you just said, "Spain is one of my favorite countries!", you'd signal, "Yeah, look at how cool I am because I travel so much." But instead, you use the open loop as kind of a throwaway detail on your way to discovering more about her. You don't focus on it, and so it doesn't come across like you're trying to impress her.

And yet it still plants the question in her mind, "What other countries has he been to?" and lays the groundwork for a deeper conversation.

Step #4: Follow the Proper Etiquette

It's not enough to know how to highlight the right qualities about yourself and bait women. You must also follow the proper etiquette for talking about yourself. Otherwise, you risk talking about yourself too much, and you come across as unattainable and damage the connection.

In terms of "talk about yourself" etiquette, there are three rules you should follow.

Rule 1: Don't make the conversation all about you.

Remember—the more she talks about herself, the more connected she'll feel to you. Therefore, she doesn't need to know all that much about you to feel like she's connected to you.

With this in mind, you shouldn't be talking about yourself for the majority of the conversation. In fact, you should keep it to a minimum. That way, she's the one talking about herself, qualifying herself to you, and really putting most of the effort in. All while you sit back, make some intriguing statements, tell a few pointed stories, and let the conversation flow.

How can you do this? After talking about yourself briefly, turn the conversation back over to her. **You can do this by:**

- **Asking her the same question she asked you.** If you've just told her what you do, you can ask her what *she* does.

- **Including her in the conversation by infusing questions about your topic.** If you tell her a story about snorkeling, you could say something like, "I *love* snorkeling—have you ever tried it?", to which she may launch into a tale about how she loves snorkeling too.

- **Asking her a random question.** You can use this as your backup plan if you feel like the conversation topic has dried up. You simply ask her a question like, "So where have you traveled to?"

Here's an example of turning the conversation back to her smoothly:

Her: "How'd you end up starting your own fitness blog?"

You: "Well, after I finished college I was pretty out of shape. One of the guys I worked with was passionate about fitness, and he got me into it. It completely enthralled me. I ended up quitting my office job to become a personal trainer, and then I thought, "How can I help more people get in shape rather than just a few clients a day?" That's why I started up my fitness blog a few years ago—to reach as many people as possible. It took a while to build traction, and a lot of people doubted me. At one point when my money was low, I even considered quitting and going back to a regular job. But I kept at it, and eventually I managed to get published on a few big sites. From there, it kept growing."

Her: "That's so interesting!"

You: "Yeah it's been quite the experience. It just seems like such a long journey when I reflect on it! What about you, though? You said you wanted to get into photography when you were younger but it never quite panned out. What stopped you from pursuing that?"

Here, you've built an interesting picture of yourself and made her curious. You haven't divulged all the details. Plus, you've given her a chance to talk even more about herself.

Rule 2: Know your "hero story."

Average is boring. Women like men who succeed in the face of adversity, overcome obstacles, and have purpose. So when you're talking about yourself, you want to convey these things.

That's where your "hero story" comes into play. The previous conversation about the fitness blog is a solid example of this.

1. He started by talking about himself when he was younger, and a goal that he had but wasn't sure how to accomplish.
2. He mentioned a few obstacles along his way to success.
3. He talked about how he began to finally see some success.
4. He talked about his ultimate success—getting published on bigger sites and growing his blog.

This is the basic hero story format. We all have multiple hero stories, so if you think on it a little bit, you can definitely come up with a few from your own life.

Maybe it was the time you got the job or promotion you didn't think you could get, or the time you made the basketball team in high school against all odds. In fact, you can make any triumph into a hero story.

These hero stories show that you're not just any average schmuck. You're the type of guy who doesn't shrink in the face of a challenge—and women love that.

Rule 3: Make it playful.

Don't paint yourself as perfect. Instead, poke some fun at your mistakes and show that you've struggled to achieve your successes despite a few mishaps along the way. It wasn't all rainbows and unicorns.

You can also add in some light-hearted playfulness. For example, going back to the fitness blog guy, he could've joked, "Hell, back in college I barely even knew what a squat was!"

So there you have it. You now know what to do to talk about yourself in an attractive way. Follow these tips and techniques, and you'll suddenly be attracting more interest from the amazing women you're interested in—the kind of women who, up until recently, might not have even given you a second look.

Key Takeaways:

- **Step #1:** Understand the purpose of talking about yourself—it's to excite and intrigue her before turning the conversation back over to her.
- **Step #2:** Highlight attractive qualities about yourself like dominance, altruism, sociability, and problem solving.
- **Step #3:** Bait her to get her more invested in the conversation and eager to know more about you.
- **Step #4:** Follow the proper etiquette so that you come across as socially savvy.

But how do you put all this together and infuse it into your conversations? One of the best ways to do it is through storytelling, and luckily, you're about to learn how to tell a kick-ass story that'll always get her hooked.

Reference:

1. Farrelly, Daniel, Paul Clemson and Melissa Guthrie. "Are Women's Mate Preferences for Altruism Also Influenced by Physical Attractiveness?" *Evolutionary Psychology* 14.1 (2016)

How to Tell a Kick-Ass Story That Hooks Her

Consider this true story that happened to me not too long ago.

I'd just stepped into my first nightclub in Vietnam after nearly 30 hours of travel. And I was scared. The music bumped and the ground shook below me. I looked around in awe.

I was with some of the guys from an entrepreneur group there. My friend introduced me to them over some drinks and hookah earlier in the night, but that didn't do much to ease my comfort level.

Sure, I loved the nightlife, but this was a whole different beast. Sleep-deprived and surrounded by unfamiliar faces, my mind raced.

I was thinking of the girl I'd just left behind in Boston—Natalie. I'd never liked a girl as much as I liked her. We'd had an amazing two months together, but I had to leave to embark on this journey, all the way across the globe.

Maybe you know the feeling. Have you ever had to leave a girl prematurely like this? It's rotten.

As I stood there for a second lost in thought, one of the guys from the entrepreneur group interrupted, "Let's go approach some girls, bro!"

He was a hyper 18-year-old local guy who was already successful in business. I was not in the mood to approach girls, but he wouldn't take no for an answer.

After a few attempted conversations, stammering through clunky English, I finally escaped to the bathroom. I walked back out to the dance floor, looked around one more time, and broke into a sweat. The weird electronic music, the crazy environment, the foreign languages…it was all too much, too fast, and I couldn't take it.

As humans, we communicate best through stories. Stories are what hook us and make us feel things.

And if you think about it, storytelling is key for most things involving people—whether it's teaching, writing, speaking, selling, leading, or attracting women.

A good story snaps people out of their boredom and captivates them. But good *storytelling*? That's hard to do, and very few people ever practice the skill. By the end of this chapter, though, you'll have all the tools you need to be able to tell great stories.

So what *is* good storytelling? Well, the "telling" part and the "story" part are two different elements. You can have all the aspects that make a good story, but if you don't tell it well, it won't be a good story. You need both pieces. And to top it off, you need to know how to tell it in a way that attracts women. We'll cover all the aspects of solid storytelling in this chapter.

The first piece is the *way* you tell the story.

To tell a story well, you should have a handle on the most important aspect of good storytelling: *you need to tell the story as if you're living it.*

You want to hold your listener's hand and walk her through every twist and turn so that she's on the edge of her seat. But how do you do that?

It's a combination of your tonality, facial expressions, and mood at each moment of your story. You want her to feel how *you* felt at the time when it was happening—not like "it's already over and everything turned out okay." Keep the sense of mystery alive.

To see some examples of this in action, I recommend checking out comedians like John Mulaney, Bill Burr, and Eugene Mirman—these guys know how to keep the mystery (and hilarity) going throughout their stories.

You can start with these clips on YouTube by John Mulaney:

- https://bit.ly/Mulaney-1
- https://bit.ly/Mulaney--2

So let's return to the story that I illustrated at the start of this chapter: How the hell did I get to that moment—stuck in an Asian nightclub, pondering life, and feeling overwhelmed?

It all started with the desire for freedom.

After graduating college with an accounting major, I soon realized that I didn't want to be an accountant; it was too boring, and I loved to create things.

When I sat in a cubicle in the accounting office, I felt caged. "This can't be all there is to life," I thought.

I was hungry for more. Hungry for adventure. I didn't want to be another guy who just checked off boxes. You know the boxes I'm talking about: go to college, get a job, buy a house, get married, have kids, buy a bigger house, get a promotion, retire, die. It all seemed so predictable—because it is.

So I saved up just enough money to quit my job and I moved back home with my parents. Even then, though, I had just enough savings to last a few months.

I had to make something happen, telling myself, "It's now or never." Scared and quickly running out of money, I did the only thing I could do—start learning.

I learned how to start a blog, and then started one. Next, I learned copywriting and tried to get clients.

The goal? Well, the long-term goal was to travel the world and achieve financial freedom. But my short-term goal was simply to make $2k a month. I knew that if I could do that, I could move to Vietnam where there were tons of location-independent entrepreneurs. (A friend of mine had been living in Vietnam for a year and raved about how he was learning so much about business and life from these entrepreneurs.)

I started off writing 500-word articles for $7.50 a pop. I remember calculating how many I needed to write per day to pay my rent. It was a lot, and certainly not sustainable. But I kept learning and looking for better opportunities.

It took me about six months and a few lucky breaks. But once I started making $2k a month, I pulled the trigger and bought my plane ticket in May of 2014. I was set to leave at the end of July.

Scared, excited, and hopeful, I knew that this could be a life-changing step on my journey. But a week after I bought my ticket, I met Natalie. She was the first girl I'd met who I could really see a future with. The problem? I knew that I'd have to leave her.

You can also make the story more interesting by involving her and pausing at the right times.

So, how do you involve her? Ask her pointed questions throughout the story that you're telling so that she feels like she's a part of it. For example, "So I was at an improv show the other night...do you like improv? Well, this was just about the funniest show I've been to. Maybe I'll take you to one sometime! Anyway, I was at this show and..."

As for pausing? Well, you should never rush through your stories—especially the important parts. You see, people don't necessarily feel moved by your words—but they always feel moved by *the spaces in between* your words. Pausing for just a second or two here and there can be powerful.

"Guys, I'm gonna head home," I told the group at the nightclub. This first night in Asia had been a little more than I'd bargained for.

I rushed out of the club and onto the street in search of a taxi. The humidity and pollution flooded my senses once again.

And that's when it hit me.

"What have I done?!" I thought.

I'd flown all the way across the world to fulfill some dream of adventure, travel, and entrepreneurship. But maybe that's not what I wanted after all.

Maybe I should've stayed in Boston and made it work with Natalie. Maybe I should've gotten a real job, made normal friends, and lived a regular life.

But I couldn't turn back. I didn't even have enough money to fly back to the USA if I wanted to!

I was on the other side of the globe, with only one person I knew in this huge city, and I had no choice but to keep going.

So I hopped in a taxi, showed the driver a little sticky note with the address written in Vietnamese, and headed back to my friend's apartment.

I wasn't sure if I'd finally gone too far—or worse, ruined my life altogether.

I texted Natalie a sappy, "Wish I was back there hanging with you," and tried to get some sleep.

The way you tell a story is important, but you also need to do it in a way that attracts women.

Let's dive into the components of the kind of story that'll attract her:

It Should Help You Connect With Her

The point of the story is to help you connect with the girl, so your stories should be about you or something that happened to you. Otherwise, they won't do much in the way of connecting.

It Should Showcase Your Attractive Qualities

Remember the qualities we covered in the last chapter? Dominance, sociability, altruism, problem solving, adventurousness, appreciation of beauty, and sense of humor, right?

These are the types of qualities you want to showcase in your stories. Don't worry about stuffing all of them into every story, but do aim to highlight two or three.

It Should Be About Something She's Interested In

This is where baiting comes into play. If she asks you about a topic relevant to your story, tell it then and not beforehand—because that's when it'll have the most impact. For example, if she asks you, "How did you end up moving to Vietnam?", that's when you can get into the nitty-gritty details with a killer story.

It Should End With a Bang

Try to end with the story with impact. You do this by wrapping everything up and having some type of takeaway.

"Hey bro, do you want to go with us?"

My friend woke me up the next morning and asked if I wanted to head over to yoga with him and the guys. I'd never tried yoga before and was still feeling very overwhelmed, but I knew that I needed some sort of pick me up.

"All right, screw it—let's do it."

I met a few more guys from the crew at this yoga session. It was an easier atmosphere to handle than the club, and I felt a little calmer and more relaxed.

Afterwards, we hit the local smoothie shop, "Juicy," to grab some post-yoga nutrition. While there, I told the guys about my experience from the night before.

"Listen," my friend began. "Being here, seeing all this, meeting these entrepreneurs—it's all overwhelming at first. I was scared for my first few months. But this is just the beginning of everything. What you're going to learn is that the world is about to open up to you. That no place is off-limits. And that there are plenty of amazing women all around the globe."

As I talked to the guys, I began to feel a bit more comfortable. They'd all been scared too when they started traveling and getting into business. And they also had similar goals of freedom, adventure, and financial success. I could relate to these guys.

Right then, I decided: "You know what? I'm going to try to make this work. I'm going to give this a shot."

Those next few weeks were tough as I become more accustomed to Asia. I still missed Natalie, and I still wasn't sure if I'd made the right decision.

But as the days passed, Vietnam grew on me more and more. I realized, "This is the type of lifestyle and freedom I've always wanted, so let me try and enjoy it."

Soon enough, I loved Vietnam and the people there. I started learning more, meeting amazing people, and having more success in business.

Ten years later, I'm living in an apartment in Mexico City, I can say for sure that it all turned out okay. Actually, more than okay. I've lived in 20 different countries since then, have made amazing friends, and built a life of complete freedom. The world has been my oyster.

If I'd retreated back home after that scary first night in Vietnam, I never would've made this amazing discovery for myself.

And while it didn't work out with Natalie, I've met so many amazing women from all around the world, deepening my perspective on life and dating.

So I guess sometimes, you have to scare yourself a little. You have to destroy your life a bit to allow for the next great thing to happen.

And that's okay. Because then you can build it back up again, better than you ever thought possible.

Obviously, I didn't tell you that story above so that you can lift it as your own—besides, you'd have to move to Mexico City so that all the details line up!

Kidding aside, the story illustrates what I'm trying to get across here—flesh out your stories with engaging detail, pause at the right moments to draw her in, and finish them off with an impactful bang.

But there's one more step to telling a story that hooks her: It needs to have a solid structure.

See, every good story should have four basic elements. And if you've been following along with my story about Vietnam, you might have picked up on them. **These elements are:**

1. **Introduction:** You introduce the characters and environment in the story to hook your listener. For example, *"I'd just stepped into my first nightclub in Vietnam after nearly 30 hours of travel. And I was scared. The music bumped and the ground shook below me. I looked around in awe."*

2. **Development.** You share the characters' main struggles and obstacles. For example, *"It took me about six months and a few lucky breaks. But once I started making $2k a month, I pulled the trigger and bought my plane ticket in May of 2014. I was set to leave at the end of July. But a week after I bought my ticket, I met Natalie. She was the first girl I ever really saw a future with. The problem? I knew I'd have to leave her."*

3. **Climax.** This is the turning point in the story. For example, *"And that's when it hit me. 'What have I done?!' I thought. I'd flown all the way across the world to fulfill some dream of adventure, travel, and entrepreneurship. But maybe that's not what I wanted after all."*

4. **Resolution.** You wind the story down and wrap it up. It's the "come down" from the climax. For example, *"I decided to give Vietnam a real try, even though it was scary. So I guess sometimes, you have to scare yourself a*

little. You have to destroy your life a bit to allow for the next great thing to happen. And that's okay. Because then you can build it back up again, better than you ever thought possible."

Key Takeaways

- **Use the Aspects of Good Storytelling:** Tell it as if you're actually living it, involve her in the story, and use effective pauses to draw her in.
- **Tell a Story That Attracts Her:** While the story needs to be engaging and exciting, it should also be about you and showcase your attractive qualities.
- **Nail the Structure:** Make sure that you're setting up your story effectively—it needs to have an introduction, some development, a climax, and an impactful resolution.

Action Tip: Write a short story about something that's happened to you, including the four elements of story structure. When you're finished, tell it aloud to yourself as if you were living it right now.

Part 6: Relationships, Compatibility & Maintaining A Masculine Frame

Casual or Serious: You Still Need a Gameplan

You now have the tools to flirt with, connect with, and attract women. What inevitably happens next, if you use the tools the right way, is that you'll have a flurry of high-quality options.

This is a good problem to have. But, as always, with great power comes great responsibility. **What this means for you is:**

- You should have a handle on your dating goals.
- You need to know how to "filter" for the women you're most excited about.
- You must correctly pace things from the first date onward to avoid "falling into" something too quickly.
- You need to assess whether different women are a good fit or not.
- You need to show up the right way within these different relationships.

When it comes to your dating goals, **the main things you need to know are the following:**

- How do you want your dating life to look short term and long term? And what's your time scale? If you want to find your future wife in the next year, that's a bit different than wanting to "play the field" for four or five years, and it requires a different approach.
- What type of women do you want to meet?

- What puts a girl in (and out) of the potential girlfriend "box?"

If you don't know the answers to all these questions just yet, that's okay. They'll become clearer as you gain more experience and figure out what you like and don't like.

For example, you may think that you want a long-term girlfriend right now. But once you start getting a few dates a week (for maybe the first time in your life), you might enjoy it and want to keep that going for a bit longer before you settle down.

Be patient with yourself, and as you figure out your goals, make sure that they're indeed *your* goals, and not just the influence of your friends and family.

All this being said, what if you just want to date casually for a few years? Do you really need to read this part of the book?

Fair question. I'll put it to you this way: I've seen many guys come into dating with this mindset, only to fall for one of the first "casual" girls they started dating without correctly assessing if she was a good fit.

What typically transpires afterwards are months or even years of wasted time in the wrong relationship. It's much better to approach this whole thing with intention, whether it's a girl you want to see casually or one you see more of a future with.

That way, if there's a "casual" girl who you're starting to see a future with, you can correctly assess and build things. Or if not, you can properly keep it casual, not lead her on, and end things at the right time.

This next part of the book will help ensure that you handle all these things optimally, spend less time with women who aren't a good fit, and lock down the right one who *is* a good fit.

Key Takeaways

- **Know Your Dating Goals:** This will help you stay on track and avoid "falling" for girls that may not be a good fit.
- **What Kind of Woman Do You Want?** Understanding this will help you meet more of the right women and steer clear of the wrong ones.

Pacing: What Most Guys Get Wrong

You have a great first date with a girl, but then what comes next?

It's easy to fumble the bag and make her lose interest at this point if you don't pace things correctly. What I mean by this is that you need to properly manage the frequency and the "depth" of your dates, especially early in the process.

What Guys Get Wrong About Pacing

"I like her, so I'm going to try to hang out with her as much as possible."

This thought goes through many guys' heads when they start seeing a girl they like. And the girl may even seem into it, too. After the first date, they both start trying to plan multiple dates a week right away.

There are a few problems with this, though.

First, it doesn't give you enough time to reflect on the connection and chemistry. Instead of taking it slow, you rush right into it. This can cause you to overlook red flags and compatibility issues that can come back to bite you later on.

Second, it makes continued growth unsustainable. You want to feel like there's a level of growth happening early on. But if, let's say two weeks in, you're already seeing her three or four times a week, it's hard to grow from there. Over time, this can cause a feeling of stagnation.

And third, it makes you seem too overeager. Think about it: Who's she going to be more attracted to long term? The guy who patiently builds things with a girl he's interested in, or the guy who dives in headfirst for a girl he barely knows?

It's much better to take it slow and gradually escalate the relationship over time.

How to Pace Things Correctly

Here's the general template you should follow for pacing:

- After the first date, aim to hang out every 7 to 10 days for a month. During this time, have your texting mainly focused on arranging date logistics.
- From there, if you're enjoying your time with her and can see potential, you can increase date frequency to two or three times a week for the next couple of months. Texting can increase a bit too, but you don't need to overdo it. You can also introduce her to your friends at this point.
- The "depth" of your dates can increase, too. Instead of hanging at home, you can go on "mini adventures," weekend trips, and other fun activities to spice things up.
- If you don't think that there's relationship potential after the first month, keep the hangouts to every 7 to 10 days max, and mainly just hang out at home. You can still enjoy casually hanging out, but if it's clear that she's looking for something more, it's better to be real with her about the situation. If she's cool with it from there, great—you can keep it casual for as long as it makes sense for the both of you. But never, ever lead a girl on.

Transitioning to a Relationship

Once you've hung out with her for two or three months and have gradually increased the dates to a few times a week, she should be very invested by this point.

So you might be thinking, "Is this the point when I should ask her to be my girlfriend?"

Here's the thing: It's far better if *she* brings up that conversation first. You want her to strongly desire the relationship—it shouldn't be something you need to "convince" her of. When she strongly desires it, the relationship starts off with a much better foundation.

And in all honesty, if she doesn't strongly desire it after two or three months, either you're doing something wrong or she's not the right fit for you (or both).

Also, it's much better to *show* her that you want her to be your girlfriend than to *tell* her. And the way that you show her is by doing exactly what was mentioned above—gradually increasing the depth and frequency of hang outs, as well as deepening the conversations and connection. If you do this, it'll be obvious for her where things are headed, and she'll inevitably bring it up (again, if she strongly desires it).

And at that point, you have an ideal situation: a woman who strongly desires to date you, who you've carefully vetted over the course of a few months, with a reasonably high probability of long-term potential.

Quick tip: As you build things up and deepen the connection over the first few months, it's a good idea to play games like "We're Not Really Strangers." This is a card game that allows you to ask fun questions and get to know her on a deeper level. They have a couples version too, and also an app (I'm not affiliated with them, by the way, but I can definitely vouch for the game).

Key Takeaways

- **Don't Screw Up the Pace:** Gradually build the depth and frequency of dates over time so that it doesn't feel rushed.
- **The 7- to 10-Day Rule:** Keep hangout frequency to once every 7 to 10 days for the first month, then gradually build from there if she seems like a good fit.
- **Avoid Leading Girls On:** If you decide that you want to keep things casual with a girl, don't treat her like you would a girlfriend. And if she seems like she wants something more, be real with her about the situation and your intentions.
- **Show Her, Don't Tell Her:** Avoid asking girls to be your girlfriend. Gradually treat her more like a girlfriend over time, and if you're doing things right, she should bring it up within two or three months.

How to Know If She's "Girlfriend Material" For You

As you pace and gradually build the budding relationship, how do you know if a girl is the right fit?

In short, you need to assess the chemistry and compatibility, so let's dive into these topics below.

The Chemistry Check

Chemistry is that electric feeling of connection you get with a girl. Every chat feels easy and never forced, there's an eagerness to get to know each other more, you're highly attracted to her (both physically and mentally), and every interaction with her gives you energy. Basically, the two of you just "click."

If this chemistry isn't on point or already feels like it's fading after a few weeks, nothing else matters: It's not going to work.

A great way to assess the chemistry a few weeks in is to do the "boring walk" test, which is exactly what it sounds like. You take a mundane walk with her somewhere, like to the grocery store or the park. Ideally, it's at least a 15- to 20-minute walk and you go on a few of them.

Do the walks feel awkward or forced? Or does conversation flow effortlessly?

The Compatibility Check

Chemistry is awesome, but without compatibility, the most that great chemistry can get you is a fun fling.

Let's look at some key things to assess in terms of compatibility.

Matching Desires for Intimacy

If one of you desires intimacy far more than the other, it can lead to feelings of rejection, pressure, and unmet needs.

It can be a little more challenging to accurately assess this early on, as couples tend to get intimate more often during the "honeymoon" phase. So, a good question to ask early on is, "When you're in a relationship, how often do you like to get intimate?" This will give you a more accurate picture, along with reading her behavior over the first few months.

Aligned Lifestyle Goals

Whether it's your career ambitions, where you want to live, or your stance on having kids, your major life goals should be in sync with one another. If you dream of a nomadic life traveling the world and she's all about settling down in her hometown, there's likely a fundamental mismatch.

This also extends to personal lifestyle choices, such as dietary habits, fitness, and how you both prefer to spend your downtime. If she wants to party every weekend but you're more of a homebody, it probably isn't going to work (unless one of you consciously decides to change).

Being clear about where you see yourselves living, how you plan to manage your finances, and your thoughts on family planning are all crucial for long-term compatibility.

Aligned Values

While you don't need to agree on everything, having core values that drastically oppose can lead to conflicts. For example, if one of you highly values independence and the other values close, constant companionship, it might cause friction.

This also applies if you're a little more on one side politically but she's on the extreme end of the other side. Liberals and conservatives can date just fine, but it's when one (or both) are on the opposite extreme ends that can make it tougher.

Conflict Resolution

How you handle disagreements is another critical compatibility factor. Do you both strive for compromise or does one tend to dominate? Are conflicts addressed head on or is there a tendency to sweep issues under the rug? A relationship in which both of you can constructively navigate conflicts will likely be more resilient and satisfying.

A key thing to look for: If she "shuts down" whenever there's a conflict or actively lashes out at you, neither of these are good signs.

Paying Attention to Red Flags

I'm not going to get into *specific* red flags here, as those will be different for every guy. But you do need to be aware of when red flags come up and look to address them. If the behavior continues even after you've addressed it, it may be time to walk away.

Of course, you won't be able to figure out all the above-mentioned things right away. It's going to take a few months of hanging out and reflecting to really get an accurate picture of how compatible you are.

This, again, is the whole reason to pace things slowly. That gives you the valuable time needed to go through this process, assess things, and avoid making rash decisions that can have long-term consequences.

Key Takeaways

- **Is She "Girlfriend Material?"** The way to truly tell is to honestly assess the chemistry and compatibility between the two of you.
- **The "Boring Walk" Test:** Do this to assess chemistry within the first few weeks. If conversation flows effortlessly, you're in good shape.
- **Testing for Compatibility:** When assessing this, reflect on values, lifestyle goals, desire for intimacy, conflict resolution preferences, and potential red flags. Be careful about overlooking something negative just because you like her.

Maintaining a Masculine Frame & Setting Boundaries

You've entered into a relationship with a beautiful woman in which there's great chemistry and compatibility. You've done it! You've beat the game and can relax and focus on other areas, right?

Well…not so fast.

See, a relationship is simply the start of a whole new game. Sure, you can rest on your laurels when it comes to getting out there, starting conversations with women, and going on lots of dates. No need to spend energy on that. But there's *still* more work to be done. One of the biggest keys to running a relationship well is to maintain a masculine frame.

The lack of a masculine frame—or you could say the "decay" of guy's masculine frame—is a common reason women lose attraction and end relationships. The guy seemed so confident coming into it, but over time, life (and perhaps even his woman) chipped away at him until he was a shell of his former self.

Imagine your masculine frame as the psychological backbone of your relationship. It's what keeps you cool under pressure, decisive when faced with choices, and clearsighted in your life's direction. It's less about being the alpha and more about being the anchor: steady, reliable, and secure. This kind of stability is magnetic—it not only sparks but sustains attraction, creating a deep, unwavering respect.

In this chapter, we'll dive into the whys and hows of maintaining your masculine frame. We'll explore how it nurtures lasting attraction, commands respect, and provides leadership in a relationship.

The Importance of a Masculine Frame

There are three key things a masculine frame helps you to do:

1. Attraction Maintenance: Keeping the Spark Alive

A masculine frame exudes a sense of stability and security. She'll see you as dependable and strong, especially in challenging situations.

As we examined before with how I resolved the opera singer situation, when a woman feels secure and stable, the attraction deepens—she values the peace of mind that comes from being with someone who can handle life's ups and downs effectively.

The masculine frame also exudes confidence. She knows that she can relax, follow your lead, and remain squarely in her femininity rather than needing to constantly take the reins because you don't know where you're going.

2. Building Respect & Admiration

Women deeply respect men who are steadfast and reliable in their masculinity. This respect isn't rooted in a fear or a power dynamic but rather in admiration for a man who knows himself and stands firm in his convictions and values.

When a woman sees that her man is unshaken by the chaos of the world, that steadiness becomes a source of security and a foundation for deep emotional connection.

3. Leading the Relationship

Maintaining a masculine frame in a relationship isn't about throwing your weight around or making all the decisions. It's about leading with a steady hand and clear intent while fully respecting her viewpoints and valuing her input.

It's about stepping up to make tough choices when necessary but doing so with consideration for the relationship's balance.

Components of a Strong Masculine Frame

Let's examine the ingredients of a strong masculine frame:

1. Self-Confidence

There are two elements to this within a relationship. The first is simply being comfortable in your own skin and not needing to seek approval or validation from others. Following the steps in both this book and Book 1 will help you to do just that.

The second element is having the ability to walk away from the relationship, knowing full well that you can create another relationship with an amazing girl if this current relationship doesn't end up working out.

If you "lucked in" to your relationship or didn't intentionally find and build it, you may lack this confidence because you have no solid strategy to replicate what you've done. That's why building an excellent dating skillset is key.

When you can walk away, you can set boundaries with strength and have more real conversations. Otherwise, it's all bravado, as you'll likely be paralyzed by the fear of loss.

2. Emotional Control

A guy who's solid in his masculine frame keeps his cool, no matter what. He's not the type to let a bad day at work or a heated argument throw him off his game. Instead, he steps back, sizes up the situation with a level head, and responds with precision—never letting his emotions get the best of him. This calmness under pressure doesn't just keep things from boiling over—it also shows that he's got the maturity to handle tough moments without breaking a sweat.

Essentially, she wants to know that you can walk through the fire and come out the other side in one piece.

3. Purpose & Direction

Rocking a strong masculine frame means that you've got your eyes on the prize—knowing exactly what you want out of life and where you're headed. It's all about setting goals and chasing ambitions, not just at work but in your personal life and within your relationship, too. This kind of clear direction means that you're not just reacting on the fly; instead, every choice is a strategic move toward the bigger picture. It steadies the ship of your relationship, letting your partner see that you're all in for the long haul and capable of building a future together.

This is also why it's incredibly ironic when guys say, "I'm going to focus on other things and let my dating life work itself out," or "The right girl will just come along…I'll let the chips fall where they may."

This attitude is, to put it bluntly, disgustingly unattractive to women. Why would she want a man who isn't willing to do the hard things to find and build the relationship he wants? She wouldn't, and so even if the right girl did "stumble along," odds are high that this type of guy will fumble the bag anyway.

4. Boundaries

Locking down your boundaries is key. It's about knowing what flies with you and what absolutely doesn't. This isn't about being tough—it's about protecting your peace and keeping your relationship solid and respectful. When you're clear on your limits, you can confidently say no or point out things that rub you the wrong way without coming off as stubborn. A guy who stands firm on his boundaries not only garners respect but also sets the standard for mutual respect in the relationship.

Let's look at some examples of setting boundaries:

Situation: She wants to ramp up the pace of hangouts too early on.

Your Boundary: Be straight up by saying, "I've learned that it's better for me to take things slowly at first. I really value what we have and want to build it on a solid foundation without needing to rush in."

Situation: Addressing repeating issues.

Your Boundary: If she keeps doing something that bugs you, after you've seen it a couple of times, bring it up. Use "I feel" statements rather than accusations. Say something like, "I feel a bit overlooked when this happens. I really appreciate open communication and it's important for me to speak up when something's on my mind."

Situation: She's constantly late.

Your Boundary: Point it out by saying something like, "It seems like you've got a lot on your plate, but I feel undervalued when our plans start late on a regular basis. I'd appreciate it if you could try to be on time."

Situation: She becomes distant or starts canceling plans.

Your Move: This isn't so much about staying firm in your boundary but more about reacting the right way. Instead of confronting her about pulling away, give her some space. She might be signaling that she needs a little room, and pushing on it could drive her further away.

If she reacts poorly when you set boundaries, stay cool and collected. Just lay it out clearly: You're big on open communication and prefer to address things directly when they're bugging you. Encourage her to adopt the same approach because it keeps everything transparent.

It's key to let her process her feelings without rushing to smooth everything over. She might get upset, and that's okay. This is when you see if she can adapt or if she resorts to less constructive behaviors, like being passive-aggressive or shutting down. Remember—how she handles this can be a telltale sign of whether she's right for the long haul.

Challenges in Maintaining Your Frame

Maintaining frame is not a "set it and forget it" kind of thing – it's an ongoing process. You'll be tested by your woman and the world, and it's on you to overcome those tests.

Dealing with Tests of Frame

Your frame will be challenged, not just once but continually. For example, she might cancel plans at the last minute to see how you'll react, or she might disagree with you on something important to see if you'll just fold and agree with her to avoid conflict. These are not just little bumps—they're actually opportunities to reinforce your frame by staying true to your values and handling the situation with calm assertiveness.

For example, let's say that she wants to hit New York City for a weekend getaway but you're more in the mood for a quiet retreat in nature.

Instead of just giving in and agreeing, you could counter: "New York sounds great, especially the food and culture you're excited about. To be honest, I'm a little 'citied out' though. What if we spend a couple of days somewhere quiet nearby, like Hudson Valley. We could enjoy some nature, and then hit the city for some food and shopping on the way back?"

This validates her preferences, asserts your own, and finds a solution that can satisfy both your interests. It shows that you respect her ideas but can also firmly communicate your needs.

Facing External Influences

You'll face pressure from friends, family, and the media—everyone seems to have an opinion on how you should run your relationship. But sticking to your guns requires you to be solid in your convictions. For instance, if your friends pressure you to prioritize hanging out over spending quality time with your partner when it's needed, you must stand firm on your commitment to balance your life and relationship in a way that aligns with your values.

Dealing with Internal Struggles

We all have our insecurities and baggage from past relationships that can shake our confidence and challenge our frame. Maybe you've been manipulated or undervalued in the past, and it's left a mark on how you view your worth in relationships. Overcoming this means working through these issues, possibly with a therapist or coach, and constantly reminding yourself of your own value, ensuring these old ghosts don't dictate your current happiness or self-esteem.

Strengthening Your Frame

The following are a few tips to dial in and strengthen your frame:

Consistent Self-Improvement

Push yourself to pick up new skills or dive into hobbies that fire you up. Whether it's learning to salsa dance, conquering a new fitness routine, or attacking a new business endeavor, these pursuits not only boost your self-esteem but also make you a more rounded, interesting guy.

Imagine striking up a conversation about your rappelling adventure or the new business you're tackling—it shows that you're a guy with drive and passion.

Work on Your Assertiveness

Assertiveness is crucial, but it's about finding the balance. Learn to express your needs clearly without tipping into aggression. This means setting boundaries respectfully and being upfront about what you're cool with and what's a no-go. If a topic like moving in together comes up and you're not ready, explain your stance without shutting down future possibilities. It's about clarity, not combativeness.

It also means learning to say no without guilt, asking for what you need in a relationship without demand, and expressing your feelings honestly when disagreements come up.

Mindfulness & Emotional Intelligence

Keeping your emotions in check through mindfulness is a game-changer. Start integrating practices like meditation or deep breathing into your daily routine to gain better control over your reactions. This isn't about suppressing feelings but managing them wisely. For example, if jealousy pops up, instead of spiraling or lashing out, take a step back, breathe, and address what's really triggering you.

Key Takeaways

- **Stability is Attractive:** Keeping a solid masculine frame builds and maintains attraction and respect.
- **Confidence and Autonomy:** The freedom to walk away reinforces your masculine frame, allowing you to establish boundaries without fear.
- **Steady at the Helm:** A man's unwavering purpose and direction give the relationship its course, avoiding the drift that comes from indecisiveness.
- **Commanding Respect:** Clear boundaries assert your value and expectations within the relationship, inviting respect rather than demanding it.
- **Balance and Flexibility:** Even the strongest frame will be tested. The key is to respond with a balanced approach, maintaining your core while valuing her input.

Final Thoughts

If you've made it this far, I congratulate you. Most people don't read all the way through books like this, and if they do, they don't take any real action on the info they've received. And that action is your next step.

As the brilliant Henry David Thoreau once wrote, "The mass of men lead lives of quiet desperation." I'll amend that to say that the mass of men lead *average* lives of quiet desperation. They lack control in most areas of their life, especially dating, which leads them to settle and feel this nagging sense of dissatisfaction.

That's why for more than a decade now, I've been so passionate about helping men with their dating. It's honestly a "gateway drug" to self-improvement. For many men, once they realize that they can conquer their fear of approaching a girl—or prove to themselves they can attract the kind of girl who they once thought was unattainable—they start thinking, "What else can I improve?"

It forces them to challenge their beliefs, think differently, and expand their comfort zone in ways they may not have never done before.

This was certainly the case for me, and it's why I went from a confused accounting major to a world-traveling entrepreneur who's helped hundreds of thousands of men across the globe. It all started with the question, "How do I talk to girls?" and kept evolving from there.

My hope for you is that this book helps you level up in a huge way—not just in dating but in every area—and puts you firmly on the path of tapping into your potential and becoming your best self.

Life is meant to be a fun adventure, and it's a hell of a lot more fun when you get to share it with beautiful, amazing women.

So if you apply what you've learned here, I can promise that you'll see big changes. You'll improve your ability to communicate, talk, and flirt with women. You'll see some satisfying results in your dating life, as well as in your ability to network with other people.

What you'll discover is that people are interesting, life is exciting, and the only limits that exist are the ones you put upon yourself.

The conversation tools in this book have helped me to live a life I once could only dream of, and it's been quite the journey.

I hope that these conversation tools help you to do the same.

So use them wisely, take some massive action, and crush it.

Epilogue: Your Dream Woman is Counting on You

You now have a complete gameplan to flirt, attract, and build a relationship with your dream woman.

You no longer need to "luck into" a great relationship. It's now in your control—as long as you can get out there and act upon what you've learned.

Get excited—the journey is just beginning, and your dream woman is counting on you to make it happen.

As we wrap things up, I want to leave you with a few additional words of wisdom to help you apply everything you've learned and become the man you're meant to be.

Don't Accept Your Excuses

There will be a million excuses that pop up when you try to improve in the areas outlined in this book (and I'm sure that some have already popped up while you've been reading), but not a single one of them is worth listening to. They're all total BS.

That's because even the best excuse in the world doesn't justify you not living the life that you're capable of.

"I'm too busy," "I'm not good looking enough," "I don't live in the right city (or country)," "I'm too short," and so on.

Okay, so what? Do it anyway. These are all obstacles that you can smash.

Value Real Connection Over Conquest

While numbers can be a sign of progress, they're not the real score.

When you look back, you might laugh about the one night stand you once had at that happy hour, or the time when you and your buddy got the prettiest girls at the bar.

But the real win is in genuine connections, moments of shared laughter, mutual understanding, and growth. It's not about notches on the belt but rather the quality of relationships you build—regardless of whether they last a lifetime or for just a meaningful chapter—and, of course, the man you become along the way.

Although, let's not kid ourselves here: You're going to have a ton of fun, too.

Constantly Cultivate Your Edge

Don't ever get complacent. There's always room to refine your edge and become sharper, more present, and more engaged with life. Whether it's through style, fitness, or wit, let your edge be something that never dulls, no matter the years or successes you accumulate.

This is true even (and especially) if you're in a long relationship. Ideally it lasts a lifetime, but in case it doesn't, you'll be fully prepared to get back out there.

The Journey *Is* the Reward

Finally, don't just focus on the endgame. Whether it's finding a partner or enjoying single life, fall in love with the experiences along the way.

When I think back to my own experiences on the "come up"—all those rejections, awkward moments, dumb things I said, wild situations I found myself in—those were some of the most fun and rewarding parts of this whole journey. They taught me about myself and what I was capable of, forcing me to level up.

And now it's your turn to take your *own* journey. So go out there and get after it.

A Parting Gift

As my way of saying thank you, I'm offering my **Dating Mastery Bundle** that includes five FREE downloads exclusive to my book readers.

Here's what you'll get:

1. **The First Date Playbook:** A cheat sheet for first date success with conversation starters, key questions to ask, and tips on creating a memorable experience.
2. **Get a Girlfriend in 30 Days - Audio Guide:** The extensive step-by-step audio guide to meeting, attracting, and dating your dream girl in 30 days or less.
3. **5 Texting Mistakes that Destroy Attraction - Audio Guide:** Discover the texting mistakes that turn her off, derail her attraction, and make you look needy.
4. **The Approach Anxiety Buster PDF:** This guide shows you exactly how to work through your anxiety and confidently start conversations with beautiful women
5. **The Top-Tier Dating Profile Kickstart:** This resource shows you how to get attractive photos and increase your matches by five to ten times on dating apps—and attract women on Instagram, too.

Download your bonuses here:

Go to daveperrotta.com/mastery or scan the QR code below.

About the Author

Dave Perrotta is a dating coach, bestselling author, and entrepreneur. He's lived in over 20 different countries and helped hundreds of thousands of men level up their dating life and find their life partners. **You can discover more dating tips from him on his podcast where he uploads three new episodes every single week:**

Just search "Dating Decoded" on your favorite podcast platform!

Can You Do Me a Favor?

Thanks for checking out my book.

I'm confident that you'll master conversation, connect with women, and flirt like a Casanova if you follow what's been written here. But before you go, I have a small favor to ask.

Might you take 60 seconds and write a quick blurb about this book on Amazon?

Reviews are the best way for independent authors (like me) to get noticed, sell more books, and spread my message to as many people as possible. I also read every review and use the feedback to write future revisions—and also future books.

Just navigate here to leave a review or scan the QR code:

mybook.to/talk-to-women

Thank you—I really appreciate your support.

Made in United States
Orlando, FL
06 July 2025

62684269R00177